MW00534772

THE PALE CRIMINAL

THE PALE CRIMINAL
PSYCHOANALYTIC PERSPECTIVES

Stephen J. Costello, Ph.D.

KARNAC

LONDON   NEW YORK

First published in 2002 by
H. Karnac (Books) Ltd.
6 Pembroke Buildings, London NW10 6RE

Copyright © 2002 Stephen J. Costello

The rights of Stephen J. Costello to be identified as the author of this work have been asserted in accordance with §§ 77 and 78 of the Copyright Design and Patents Act 1988.

All rights reserved. No part of this publication may be reproduced, stored in a retrieval system, or transmitted, in any form or by any means, electronic, mechanical, photocopying, recording, or otherwise, without the prior written permission of the publisher.

British Library Cataloguing in Publication Data

A C.I.P. for this book is available from the British Library

   ISBN 1 85575 295 6

10 9 8 7 6 5 4 3 2 1

Edited, designed, and typeset by The Studio Publishing Services Ltd, Exeter

www.karnacbooks.com

I would like to dedicate this book to my good friend, Oisín Quinn, with deep affection and admiration

"If the little savage were left to himself, preserving all his foolishness and adding to the small sense of a child in the cradle the violent passions of a man of thirty, he would strangle his father and lie with his mother".

Diderot, *Le Neveau de Rameau.*

"The lights jig in the river
With a concertina movement
And the sun comes up in the morning
Like barley-sugar on the water
And the mist on the Wicklow hills
Is close, as close
As the peasantry were to the landlord,
As the Irish to the Anglo–Irish,
As the killer is close one moment
To the man he kills,
Or as the moment itself
Is close to the next moment".

Louis MacNeice, *Closing Album.*

"The man had killed the thing he loved,
And so he had to die.

Yet each man kills the thing he loves,
By each let this be heard,
Some do it with a bitter look,
Some with a flattering word,
The coward does it with a kiss,
The brave man with a sword".

Oscar Wilde, *The Ballad of Reading Gaol.*

CONTENTS

ABBREVIATIONS

S.E.   *The Standard Edition of the Complete Psychological Works of Sigmund Freud*

CW   *The Collected Works of C. G. Jung*

ACKNOWLEDGEMENTS

I would like to thank the editor of *The Letter: Lacanian Perspectives on Psychoanalysis* for permission to reproduce my article "The Pale Criminal: A Freudian Perspective" which appeared in the Autumn edition of 1997 (issue 11) and which appears here as chapter one. My thanks also to the editor of *The Journal of the Irish Forum for Psychoanalytic Psychotherapy* for permission to reprint my article entitled "Klein's Little Criminals" in the Spring edition of the journal in 1998 and which appears here as chapter three.

My deep gratitude to all my friends and family as well as my colleagues in the Association for Psychoanalysis and Psychotherapy in Ireland, without whom this present work would simply not have been written.

"You do not intend to kill, you judges and sacrificers, before the beast has bowed its neck? Behold, the pale criminal has bowed his neck: from his eye speaks the great contempt. 'My Ego is something that should be overcome: my Ego is to me the great contempt of man' ... But the thought is one thing, the deed is another ... An image made this pale man pale. He was equal to his deed when he did it: but he could not endure its image after it was done ... the blow he struck charmed his simple mind ... Thus says the scarlet judge: 'Why did this criminal murder? He wanted to steal'. But I tell you: his soul wanted blood and not booty: he thirsted for the joy of the knife! ... And now again the lead of his guilt lies upon him, and again his simple mind is so numb, so paralysed, so heavy. If only he could shake his head his burden would roll off: but who can shake his head? ... This poor soul interpreted to itself what this body suffered and desired—it interpreted it as lust for murder and greed for the joy of the knife ... Much about your good people moves me to disgust, and it is not their evil I mean. How I wish they possessed a madness through which they could perish, like the pale criminal ... Thus spake Zarathustra".

Nietzsche, "Of The Pale Criminal", *Zarathustra's Discourses.*

The criminal

The effect the criminal exerts upon us is always one of fascinated horror, reflecting as he does the criminal in all of us (see David Dixon, 1986). As Ferenczi states: "I must look for the cause of my own repressed criminality. To some extent I admire the man who dares to do the things I deny to myself" (1985, p. 196). And as Jung puts it: "We are all potential murderers" (*CW* 2, p. 453). By inducing punishment, the pale criminal purges the sense of guilt from which he suffers (see Freud, 1923, p. 52). "Projection" is thus a way of dealing with unconscious guilt. The criminal commits forbidden actions precisely because they are forbidden, and in so doing obtains mental relief, as Freud noted. Suffering from a severe superego, the pale criminal embarks on his course of action in order to allay this burden of guilt. The actions rationalise the guilt and, by incurring punishment, they offer the guilt a way of dissipating itself. The guilt can thus be purged and rationalised simultaneously. Freud traced the origin of this sense of guilt back to incestuous and murderous impulses entertained at the Oedipal phase. As Glover notes:

> The perfectly normal infant is almost completely egocentric, greedy, dirty, violent in temper, destructive in habit, profoundly sexual in purpose ... In fact, judged by adult standards, the normal boy is for all practical purposes a born criminal [1960, p. 8].

Guilt, then, precedes and explains rather than succeeds and is explained by the crimes pale criminals commit (see Richard Wollheim, 1988, p. 4). We can call criminals from a sense of guilt "pale criminals", as Freud, following Nietzsche, called them. However, Nietzsche thought that there were also "rosy" types of criminals, who do not possess any guilt, conscious or unconscious, a point that Jung picks up. An ethical question to be addressed is: As a condition, is *pale criminality* an excuse? Richard Wollheim answers this question in the affirmative (ibid., p. 15). Culturally, however, there would be resistances to this conclusion due to our defences against our own repressed criminal impulses. As Reik writes in *The Unknown Murderer*:

> The horror of the crime, the desire for expiation, the urgent need to

find the culprit, all these bear witness to a defence against our own repressed impulses ... The countertendency, strengthened by reaction, finds an outlet in the wish to find and punish the culprit [1936, pp. 236–237].

And as William A. White points out in *Insanity and the Criminal Law*:

> The criminal becomes the scapegoat upon which he [man] can transfer his own tendency to sinfulness and thus by punishing the criminal he deludes himself into feeling a religious righteous indignation, thus bolstering up his own self-respect and serving in this roundabout way, both to restrain himself from like indulgences and to keep himself upon the path of cultural progress. The legal punishment of the criminal today is, in its pathology, a dramatic tragic action by which society pushes off its criminal impulses upon a substitute [1923, pp. 13–14].

Freud himself, in "The Expert Opinion in the Halsmann Case", makes a similar ethical point when he states: "Precisely because it is always present, the Oedipus complex is *not* to provide a decision on the question of guilt" (1931, p. 252) (my italics). He goes on to say that an interpretation of guilt may be true psychologically but the unconscious motivation must not be the decisive factor in pronouncing judgement. As Reik opines: "The problem is to lead the criminal to a recognition of his guilt in the psychological sense ('Do you recognise that you're guilty?') and not in the legal sense ('Do you admit being guilty?')" (1936, p. 158).

Pale and rosy criminals

We mentioned above "pale" and "rosy" criminality. Just how many forms of criminality are there? According to Lacanian theory, there are *three* nosologically and morphologically distinct clinical structures: neurosis (hysteria, phobias and obsessional neurosis), psychosis (paranoid schizophrenia and manic-depressive psychosis) and the perversions (sadomasochism, voyeurism, exhibitionism, fetishism etc. Homosexuality is *not* regarded as a perversion). Applying Lacanian theory to criminality, I would want to argue here that there are *three* forms of criminality, *structurally* speaking.

The criminal can be a neurotic, psychotic or perverse subject. *Pale criminals* are either *neurotic* criminals (for example, perhaps a thief) or *perverse* criminals (a criminal who engages in perverse acts). A *rosy criminal* (a term I borrow from Nietzsche), on the other hand, is a *psychotic* criminal (for example, some serial killers), as psychotic subjects possess no guilt, though they may experience shame. Needless to say, to make a diagnosis as to structure, one would need to know more of their story and their suffering. In my view, there should not be a separate clinical category for delinquency, as some French Lacanians are arguing for. So, this work concerns itself with *pale* and not with rosy criminals.

The pale criminal is in pain and needs to be understood. However, to understand is not, necessarily, to excuse. Our prison system should be both retributive and rehabilitative, incorporating both punishment as well as psychotherapy. Of course, many individuals have been regarded as criminals by the positive law of the state. We think of Socrates, Christ and Thomas Moore, whose names and deeds have echoed down the centuries. They remained true to another law, which Thomists would refer to as the natural law, Kierkegaardians as the involvement of a "teleological suspension of the ethical", and Lacanians as being in touch with the law of desire. In this last regard, we can point to the majestic figure of Antigone who embodied an ethics of desire, as Lacan persuasively argued.

It is the concentration, though, upon *psychoanalytic theory* rather than legal, moral, medical, philosophical, psychiatric or sociological research that distinguishes this present work. Perhaps this is the only reason to justify yet another addition to the extensive literature dealing with criminality, which I have no wish to reduplicate. It is, in my opinion, sufficient reason. My modest hope is that this book will, at least, stimulate reflection and contribute to the current widespread debate on the contemporary social question of criminality. Such is my hermeneutic wager.

Structure of the book

This work is a study of the aetiology and phenomenology of "pale criminality" from divergent psychoanalytic perspectives. A theory of criminality is proposed based on a psychoanalytic model of the human subject. My aim in writing this book is, for the first time, to correlate the major psychoanalytic writings on criminality scattered throughout the corpus of the works of Sigmund Freud, Carl Jung, Melanie Klein, Donald Winnicott and Jacques Lacan, while also including the contribution of both orthodox and evolutionary psychiatry. I also include a substantial section on the family and discuss its effects on the structure of the pale criminal.

There have been innumerable works written on criminality drawing upon psychological, psychiatric, legal and sociological sources, which purport to explain the root causes of crime. However, one major caveat must be issued on these contemporary studies on criminality, and that is; they remain at the level of consciousness and as such, in my view, are as superficial as they are myopic. For in order to understand and gain psychological insight into criminality, it is necessary to address and adduce the *unconscious*, psychoanalytical factors involved. In short, depth-psychological considerations are lacking in the above accounts. This work attempts to redress the balance in explicating the unconscious configurations pertaining to pale criminality and its myriad modalities. This book, then, is an account of the application of psychoanalytic theories to pale criminality.

I will seek to apply the theoretical, practical and profound contributions of psychoanalysis to pale criminality. Psychoanalysis deepens our knowledge of human beings through its emphasis on the unconscious motives governing human behaviour, not through experimentation and measurement, but through an appreciation of the speaking subject. This book draws on the discoveries and unique insights of psychoanalysis through discussing the major writings of those theoreticians and clinicians who have written extensively on this subject. In so doing, this book will also serve as an introduction to the main themes and tenets of psychoanalytic theory as represented by Freud, Jung, Klein, Winnicott and Lacan. One word in relation to this: the reader will, of course, be aware that Jung's school of depth-psychology is known as "analytical psychology" and not "psychoanalysis", thus distinguishing it from its Freudian counterpart. However, it is solely for reasons of convenience that I have placed Jung in the psychoanalytic domain. It would be stylistically cumbersome and repetitive to have to constantly refer to "psychoanalysis and analytical psychology" throughout. Moreover, this decision seems justified as there are four psychoanalysts being represented compared to one analytical psychologist—Jung himself. No slight whatsoever is intended and I beg the reader's indulgence in this respect.

This present work is intended for all those interested in both criminality and psychoanalysis and I hope that it will be of benefit to analysts, of all schools, academic psychologists and psychiatrists, as well as to lawyers, magistrates, legal scholars, moral philosophers, sociologists and interested laymen. Equally, it should be helpful to all those students, both undergraduate and postgraduate, who are engaged in psychoanalytic, analytical psychological and criminological research.

My emphasis throughout the first five chapters is on exposition, while critical commentary and exegesis will be the main focus in chapters six and especially chapter seven. In that chapter I will aim at a dialectical synthesis in which I will summarise, discuss, develop, compare, contrast, analyse and evaluate the insights gleaned from the preceding chapters. The concluding chapter thus offers a unifying vision and theoretical integration of the melange of different theoretical orientations.

In researching and writing this book, I have been struck by the fact that the theses offered by the psychoanalysts included in this work represent complementary rather than contradictory attempts to comprehend the phenomenon of pale criminality. Each angle covered corrects and modifies the shortcomings of the others. All the theorists I have considered here have, through their divergent points of departure and differing emphases and biases, contributed something novel and significant to our understanding and appreciation of the clinical field of pale criminality. Each adds a new and important facet to the topic and, in doing so, not only enriches but also ameliorates it. Needless to say, purists from each analytical school may find themselves perplexed by the dialectical synthesis this book is struggling towards, but this multi- dimensional approach is, I would argue, precisely the book's strength.

One outstanding feature of the analytical "community", as well as the academic world, is that far too frequently each representative section keeps their theoretical formulations confined amongst themselves. There is no real authentic exchange of information and ideas, no open receptivity. To a greater or lesser extent, each analytic school is guilty of this intellectual incest. As a result, no radical and rigorous questioning takes place, no rational and stimulating reflection, no critique of prevailing presumptions and preconceptions.

I hope this present work overcomes such professional provinciality and partisanship, which has polarised and stultified our contemporary intellectual climate. My approach here is a comparative one of cross-fertilisation. I welcome a dialogue, as in *dia-leigen* (to welcome the difference), while avoiding a facile eclecticism, believing critical dialogue and creative dispute to be deeply rewarding and in keeping with the dialectical and metaxological conception of life, which the great sages in the history of humankind have advocated and embraced.

Due to the limitations necessarily imposed upon any book, I intend to confine my analytic theorising to the works of Sigmund Freud, Carl Gustav Jung, Melanie Klein, Donald Winnicott and Jacques Lacan. I realise that this inevitably involves omitting other significant psychoanalytic theorists from the object-relations school (see Otto Fenichel, 1928 and Betty Joseph, 1960) and the speculations of the ego-psychologists (see Nathan Hale, 1995), but this research is meant only as an outline and is, hence, approximate. However, I hope to have adequately highlighted some pervasive and central concepts pertaining to the hitherto much psychoanalytically unexamined area of pale criminality.

This book, then, contains within itself the promise of future developments, and holds the hope for future original research and theoretical as well as clinical riches. Without presuming to be complete or exhaustively articulated, this analysis aims only at investigating pale criminality from the seminal standpoint of Freudian, Jungian, Kleinian, Lacanian and psychiatric interpretations. Certain questions will, inevitably, remain unanswered.

To this end, in chapter one I will adumbrate Freud's classical interpretations of pale criminality, which he understood to be due to the externalisation of unconscious guilt. Though references to pale criminality by Freud can be found in the most unlikeliest of places, all of which will be drawn upon, particular attention will be paid to the following works which deal explicitly with our topic: "Psycho-Analysis and the Establishment of the Facts in Legal Proceedings" (1906), "Some Character Types Met with in Psycho-Analytic Work"

(1916), "The Economic Problem of Masochism" (1924), "Preface to Aichorn's 'Wayward Youth'" (1925), "Dostoevsky and Parricide" (1928), "The Expert Opinion in the Halsmann Case" (1931) and "The Dissection of the Psychical Personality" (1933).

Jung's writings on pale criminality are the subject matter of chapter two, which I will begin by outlining a brief account of the analytical psychology he founded. I will then proceed to discuss the connection between criminality and the word association tests employed by Jung early on in his career as a psychiatrist in order to uncover various unconscious complexes. I will then give an account of the relevant sections of Jung's seminar on Nietzsche's *Thus Spake Zarathustra* in which he sets out his analytical insights on pale criminality. After which, I will apply Jung's conceptualisations on the "shadow" to criminality and show how the criminal subject is acting under the spell of the shadow which he has failed to consciously assimilate. To this end, the following works are consulted: "The Psychological Diagnosis of Evidence", *Experimental Researches* (CW 2); "The Association Method" (CW 2); "New Aspects of Criminal Psychology: Contribution to the Method Used for the Psychological Diagnosis of Evidence *(Tatbestandsdiagnose)*" (CW 2); "Crime and the Soul" (1932), *The Symbolic Life: Miscellaneous Writings* (CW 18); *Memories, Dreams, Reflections; The Undiscovered Self: Present and Future* (CW 10); *Nietzsche's Zarathustra: Notes of the Seminar Given In 1934–1939 by C. G. Jung; Aion: Researches into the Phenomenology of the Self* (CW 9, pt. ii); and *Civilization In Transition* (CW 10).

Chapter three will be devoted to Melanie Klein's conceptualisations on pale criminality. Again, I will begin with a synopsis of key Kleinian concepts before discussing her central hypothesis: that the crimes committed by adults often resemble the unconscious phantasy wishes of children. Klein believed that a process of externalisation into play or actual crime may occur as a way of mitigating the internal violence between instinctual impulses on the one hand, and the prohibitions of the superego on the other. Klein's researches confirmed Freud's view that criminal tendencies result from an internal situation of guilt arising from a very severe superego. Her contributions will be explored in detail both in their comparisons with and departures from the classical Freudian position, particularly her point that the criminal can possess a crushing conscience. Numerous clinical case histories from her work are included as examples. The works I shall consider, which deal explicitly with pale criminality, are: "Criminal Tendencies in Normal Children" (1927), "The Early Development of Conscience in the Child" (1933) and "On Criminality" (1934). However, references will also be made to the following works as they relate to our subject: *The Psychoanalysis of Children* (1932), "Envy and Gratitude" (1957) and "Some Reflections on *The Oresteia*" (1963).

Winnicott follows Klein in chapter four. After citing innumerable examples of his work and experiences with delinquents and children during the Second World War in Britain, I will examine his central insight: that delinquency is inextricably interlinked with (emotional) deprivation. His papers on this aspect of his work deal with the connection between delinquency and deprivation, the childhood roots of aggression, the capacity for concern, the deprivation complex and the psychological aspects of, what Winnicott terms, the "anti-social tendency", as well as the practical management of delinquent children; and most of these have been collected and published in a volume entitled *Delinquency and Deprivation* (1984), which will be explored in detail.

This will be followed, in chapter five, by Lacan's perspective on pale criminality. In Lacan's view, the criminal acts in the Real order in a symbolic manner. As such, Lacan's epistemological triad of the Real, the Symbolic and the Imaginary registers of human existence will be explained. In his 1962–1963 seminar on *Anxiety* and in his 1967–1968 seminar *The Psychoanalytic Act*, Lacan makes a crucial distinction between acting-out and *passage à l'acte*, which is often associated with paranoia and violent crime and can point to an acute psychotic episode, which will be discussed in detail. We will draw on Lacan's reflections on Freud's case history, "The Psychogenesis of a Case of Homosexuality in a Woman" (Freud, 1920, pp. 145–172), and the case of Aimée, who attacked an actress with a knife, as examples of the *passage à l'acte*. It is in his recently translated paper in the *Écrits* entitled "Introduction théorique aux fonctions de la psychanalyse en criminologie" (1950), translated as "A Theoretical Introduction to the Functions of Psychoanalysis in Criminology" (1996), that Lacan sets out his psychoanalytic interpretation of pale criminality, the central themes of which will be expounded.

Chapter six examines the contribution of both orthodox and evolutionary psychiatry to "the antisocial personality disorder", a generic term covering criminality, the diagnostic criteria of which is drawn from the *D.S.M. IV*. The main themes in evolutionary psychiatry are outlined, guided by the recent work of Anthony Stevens and John Price, as recorded in their book *Evolutionary Psychiatry: A New Beginning* (1996) and applied to the "antisocial personality disorder". I will make connections between this work and the "attachment theory" of John Bowlby, as well as Jung's theory of archetypes. I will also draw on an early work of Lacan's entitled *Family Complexes in the Formation of the Individual* (1938). Then I will summarise the sociological and biological findings of psychiatry in relation to the "antisocial personality disorder". And I will end with a Lacanian critique of the medical model of mind, utilising Lacan's "discourse theory", which makes the point that psychiatry embodies a "master discourse". This pays little or no attention to the involvement of *unconscious*, psychodynamic factors, which are the primary focus and proper concern of this present study.

The final chapter, chapter seven, aims at a dialectical synthesis of all the psychoanalytical perspectives on pale criminality covered in this work, teasing out the various viewpoints, synthesising the findings, comparing and contrasting the insights, evaluating and appraising them and emphasising their respective and relative strengths and weaknesses. I will begin with a philosophical and psychoanalytic discussion of the nature, function and relevance of "dialectics", a respectable Hegelian pedigree, and apply this procedure to the discoveries yielded by psychoanalysis on the subject of pale criminality, and I will conclude with a list of *seven* psychodynamic criteria pertaining to the pale criminal and his structure.

In the concluding note, I will add my own succinct musings and some aphoristic reflections on the subject of the pale criminal's structure.

I have written each chapter from the particular standpoint of the theorist in question. To take an example, the chapter on Jung has been written from a Jungian point of view in so far as I do not set out to critique certain central concepts, such as archetypes. This holds for all the chapters. I have attempted to be fair to each analytical school that is represented. That said, my own orientation is Freudian–Lacanian. What I offer here is a repertoire rather than a received or recognised dogma.

CHAPTER ONE

Freud: a need for punishment

"I moved forward ... And this time, without sitting up, the Arab drew his knife and held it out towards me in the sun. The light leapt up off the steel and it was like a long, flashing sword lunging at my forehead ... It was like a red-hot blade gnawing at my eyelashes and gouging out my stinging eyes. That was when everything shook. The sea swept ashore a great breath of fire. The sky seemed to be spitting from end to end and raining down sheets of flame. My whole being went tense and I tightened my grip on the gun. The trigger gave, I felt the underside of the polished butt and it was there, in that sharp but deafening noise, that it all started. I shook off the sweat and the sun. I realized that I'd destroyed the balance of the day and the perfect silence of this beach where I'd been happy. And I fired four more times at a lifeless body and the bullets sank in without leaving a mark. And it was like giving four sharp knocks at the door of unhappiness"

Albert Camus, *The Outsider*

I n this chapter, I wish to set out Sigmund Freud's (1856–1939) psychoanalytic interpretations of pale criminality, which are scattered throughout the corpus of his works. We shall see that for Freud pale criminality expresses the externalisation of unconscious guilt and the attendant need for punishment. As such, it is intimately interconnected with the superego and thus the Oedipus complex.

Secrets: neurotic and criminal

In "Psycho-Analysis and the Establishment of the Facts in Legal Proceedings" (1906), Freud draws parallels between the pale criminal and the hysteric. Both personality structures are concerned with a secret, with keeping something hidden. Freud maintains that the pale criminal knows his secret whereas the hysteric hides it even from himself. According to Freud, repressed psychical material generates psychosomatic and physiological symptomatology, which plagues the patient in the same manner as a guilty conscience disturbs the pale criminal. The analyst, like the examining magistrate, has to uncover and unearth this hidden psychical material utilising a number of detective devices in order to do so, the main one being free-association. The spontaneous thoughts that emerge from free-association will not be arbitrary but determined by their relation to this hidden secret. Of course, the patient may show signs of resistance, which is a sign that the thoughts relate to the complex in question. He may hesitate, pause, stutter or keep silent. Hidden, unconscious meanings can be glimpsed or glanced through these rifts or ruptures in the text of his speech, in the gaps and gaffes of his spoken discourse. Secrets betray themselves through subtle and ambiguous allusions (ibid. pp. 108–109).

The difference between the two structures is that the neurotic is genuinely ignorant of the secret, whereas the pale criminal will pretend to be ignorant. Furthermore, the neurotic patient will consciously assist in any effort to combat his resistance; the pale criminal will not. If the resistance in the psychoneuroses arises in the frontier between the unconscious and consciousness, in the case of the pale criminal one can say that the resistance comes from consciousness. Another feature which distinguishes the neurotic from the pale criminal is that the former is repressing a sexual complex, according to Freud, whereas the latter is not (ibid., pp. 111–112). The question is this: is conscious resistance betrayed in the same way and by the same indicators as unconscious resistance?

Freud's answer is in the negative. The complication is due to this fact: the innocent neurotic reacts as if he were guilty due to a sense of guilt *already present* in him which seizes upon the particular instance. This is because he may have committed a *prior* crime of which he is not being accused and about which his lawyer knows nothing. As Freud puts it: "He therefore quite truthfully denies being guilty of the one misdeed, while at the same time betraying his sense of guilt on account of the other. In this respect—as in so many others—the adult neurotic behaves just like a child" (ibid., p. 113).

In the three essays that comprise "Some Character Types Met with in Psychoanalytic Work" (1916), Freud further expounds this notion of unconscious guilt, which is so important for understanding the pale criminal's mind. Indeed the third essay is entitled: "Criminals from a Sense of Guilt". It is in this paper that Freud first sets out the close connection between the sense of guilt and the Oedipus complex.

According to Freud, so-called respectable persons often engage in forbidden actions such as fraud, theft and arson, to give some examples (ibid. p. 332). The reason for this is that they bring mental relief for the perpetrator. Freud explicitly relates this to their sense of guilt. "He was suffering from an oppressive feeling of guilt, of which he did not know the origin, and after he had committed a misdeed this oppression was mitigated" (ibid.). What is important to note here is that the sense of guilt was present *prior* to the misdeed. According to Freud, the sense of guilt does not arise from the misdeed but conversely the misdeed arises from the sense of guilt. These are the people that Freud calls "criminals from a sense of guilt" (ibid.). He makes the same point in his work, *The Ego and the Id* (1923) where he writes:

> It was a surprise to find that an increase in this Ucs. sense of guilt can turn people into criminals. But it is undoubtedly a fact. In many criminals, especially youthful ones, it is possible to detect a very powerful sense of guilt which existed before the crime, and is therefore not its result but its motive. It is as if it was a relief to be able to fasten this unconscious sense of guilt on to something real and immediate [p. 52].

Guilt induces them to seek punishment, just as naughty children seek and provoke punishment, after which they become quiet and content. This, then, is the motive for their misdeeds. However, even if it is the vast majority of criminals that are thus motivated, some criminals have no sense of guilt (possess no moral inhibition), according to Freud (1916, p. 333). In my view, these would be "rosy" criminals. The two questions Freud poses are: What exactly is the origin of this obscure sense of guilt, and is it probable that this plays a considerable part in the commission of crime?

The first great crime

Let us attempt to answer these crucial questions. According to Freud this obscure sense of guilt derives from the Oedipus complex and is a reaction "to the two great criminal intentions of killing the father and having sexual relations with the mother" (ibid.). Crimes are committed to allay this guilt, which comes as a relief to those (suffering) criminals. So Freud does seem to be saying that a sense of guilt plays a substantial role in crime. For Freud, the two great crimes with which humanity began were patricide and incest with the mother, which is the main theme of Freud's *Totem and Taboo* (1912–1913), to which we will now turn our attention.

In this work Freud relies on evolutionary biologists and upon ethnopsychological explanations and psychohistorical averrals in order to arrive at his conclusions about the origins of religious belief. Though the work contains many interesting insights, it has been largely dismissed by anthropologists. Together with *The Future of an Illusion* (1927) and *Moses and Monotheism* (1939), *Totem and Taboo*, whose subtitle is *Some Points of Agreement Between the Mental Lives of Savages and Neurotics*, represents one of Freud's main treatises on religion. The text is divided into four parts: the first essay deals with incest, the second with taboo prohibitions as a whole, the third treats of animism and magic, while the fourth looks at totemism itself. Throughout all the essays, Freud finds a similarity between customs, conventions and religious rites and rituals of primitive peoples on the one hand and the obsessive patterns of his neurotic patients on the other hand. Ultimately, what Freud wanted was to produce a psychogenesis of religious belief.

Freud begins by asserting that totemism was prevalent amongst the primitive peoples in such places America, Africa and Australia. A totem is an object that a savage regards with superstitious respect. It can be a plant or, more commonly, an animal that stands in a peculiar relation to the whole clan, protecting the man while he in turn promises not to kill it. Drawing heavily for his sources on the theories of Sir James Frazer, Freud maintained that even the most highly developed races underwent the stage of totemism, which is seen by Freud as the foundation of religion itself. His commentary, necessarily condensed, runs as follows: originally, primaeval man lived in primal hordes (accepting the Darwinian hypothesis of the primitive horde), dominated by one single male, the father, who jealously coveted the females in the clan for himself. One day, the band of brothers decided to supplant the father by slaying him and, being cannibals, they ate him. As Freud puts it:

> One day, the brothers who had been driven out came together, killed and devoured their father and so made an end of the patriarchal horde ... the totem meal ... would thus be a repetition and a commemoration of this memorable and criminal deed, which was the beginning of so many things—of social organization, of moral restrictions and of religion [1912–1913, pp. 141–142].

Freud informs us that psychoanalysis reveals that a man's feelings toward his father are always ambiguous and ambivalent, an admixture of love as well as hate (the Oedipus complex). So that, after the murder, the brothers' hatred for the father vanished and each, instead, experienced remorse. "They hated their father, who presented such a formidable obstacle to their craving for power and their sexual desires; but they loved and admired him too" (ibid., p. 143). After they had murdered him, "a sense of guilt made its appearance" (ibid.). In order to expiate their communal guilt and to atone for the collective murder, they prohibited the killing of the totem animal, which was the symbol of the father and they agreed to renounce relations with the father's former females by proclaiming the prohibition of incest and imposing exogamy. "They revoked their deed by forbidding the killing of the totem, the substitute for their father; and they renounced its fruits by resigning their claim to the women who had now been set free. They thus created out of their filial sense of guilt, the two fundamental taboos of totemism" (ibid.).

These two taboos (killing the totem and marrying inside one's clan) correspond to the two aspects of the Oedipus complex, namely, the killing of the father and the taking of the mother as a wife and are the basis of morality, religion and social organisation. As Freud states: "I want to state the conclusion that the beginning of religion, ethics, society and art meet in the Oedipus complex" (ibid., p. 156). This, of course, condenses centuries of primaeval life. The brothers, in community, determined never to repeat the "deed" (the primal murder) except in commemoration of the original deed, which took the form of a feast. An animal (the totemic creature), as a symbol of the father whom they had hated and loved, was slaughtered for their satiation. Totemism is thus seen as the precursor to the later development of religion. The filial remorse, resulting in mandatory exogamy and the prohibition on parricide, turned the parent of the primal horde into a God by an act of expiatory deification.

In thus relating totemism to religion, Freud describes how the sons "could attempt in their relation to this surrogate father [totem], to allay their burning sense of guilt, to bring about a kind of reconciliation with their father" (ibid. p. 144). Totemic religion grew from the attempt to allay the filial sense of guilt. Religion is, thus, an attempt to resolve the original problem posed by the murder and its ensuing guilt. The consequences of Freud's psychoanalytic and phylogenetic considerations and construals of our prehistory are reflected, in his view, in neurosis in the individual and in religion in the species. Furthermore, Freud holds that each of us carries the cumulative memory of these phyloge-netic events in our unconscious, the psychological nucleus of them bringing the Oedipus complex. Shortly before his own death, Freud announced in "Moses and Monotheism" that "men have always known that they once possessed a primal father and killed him" (1939, p. 101).

Freud's concluding words in *Totem and Taboo* are as reminiscent of the words in St. John's Gospel as they are of a saying by Goethe in *Faust*, which Freud was fond of quoting: "In the beginning was the Deed" (1912–1913, p. 161). Humanity thus began with the criminal deed of murder and developed with an attendant sense of guilt and the masochistic unconscious need for punishment to which it gave rise.

Moral masochism and unconscious guilt

In "The Economic Problem of Masochism" (1924b), Freud connects this unconscious sense of guilt to moral masochism and so we shall now consider this paper. For Freud, masochism is a counterpart of sadism (and vice versa); there is always a fusion and confusion of these two instincts, which never appear in pure form. There is always an amalgamation, therefore, between the libidinal life instincts governed by the pleasure principle and the destructive or death instincts governed by the Nirvana principle. In this respect, primal sadism, as a manifestation of the death instinct, can be equated with masochism, which comes in *three* forms, according to Freud. These are: an erotogenic masochism (a condition imposed on sexual excitation—pleasure in pain), a feminine masochism (for Freud, an expression of the feminine nature) and a moral masochism (a norm of behaviour connected with unconscious guilt). Freud holds that a sense of guilt finds expression in the manifest content of masochistic phantasies. The Lacanian notion of *jouissance*, by which I mean the pleasure inherent in pain, may be encountered in primary erotogenic masochism. Here the subject assumes he has committed some crime that needs to be expiated by a painful procedure. In feminine masochism, the impotent subject's phantasies terminate in an act of masturbation or alternatively they represent sexual satisfaction in themselves. The performance of those perverts who are also masochistic accords with these phantasies of being gagged, bound, beaten, whipped, derided and debased. The masochist wishes to be treated like a naughty child. Such phantasies place the subject in the female situation and signify being castrated or copulated with. In the case of moral masochism it is suffering itself that matters, but not necessarily inflicted by the loved object or endured at his command. "The true masochist always turns his cheek whenever he has a chance of receiving a blow" (ibid., p. 165).

Freud here maintains that it is incorrect to speak of an "unconscious" sense of guilt, as feelings cannot properly be described as "unconscious". Instead, he offers the term "need for punishment" for our consideration (ibid. p. 166). Moral masochists are dominated by morally inhibited and sensitive consciences, whose needs are satisfied by suffering and punishment at the hands of a parental power. According to Freud, masochism or the turning of sadism against the subject, is due to cultural suppression of the death instincts and "the suppression of an instinct can ... result in a sense of guilt and ... a person's conscience becomes more severe and more sensitive the more he refrains from aggression against others" (ibid., p. 170).

Consciousness of guilt is an expression of the tension between the ego and the superego. "The ego reacts with feelings of anxiety (conscience anxiety) [*Gewissenangst*] to the perception that it has not come up to the demands made by its ideal, the superego" (ibid. p. 167). The superego (Kant's categorical imperative), which is formed upon layers of unconscious identifications with introjects from early childhood, is the heir of the Oedipus complex. The first objects of the id's libidinal impulses to become internalised into the ego are parents mostly, or other such significant others. The superego is then the substitute for the Oedipus complex and the source of our moral sense. In lecture xxi of his *Introductory Lectures on Psycho-Analysis* (1916–1917) entitled "The Development of the Libido and the Sexual Organisations", Freud views the Oedipus complex as one of the most important sources of this sense of guilt by which neurotics are tormented. He writes that "Mother-incest was one of the crimes of Oedipus, parricide was the other" (ibid. p. 335) and he gives an apt quotation from Diderot's *Le Neveau de Rameau*, translated into German by Goethe, which can be rendered into English thus: "If the little savage were left to himself, preserving all his imbecility and adding to the small sense of a child in the cradle the violent passions of a man of thirty, he would strangle his father and lie with his mother" (ibid. p. 338).

Dostoevsky

In "Dostoevsky and Parricide" (1928), Freud further explores the inter-related themes of masochism, the sense of guilt and the Oedipus complex. He begins by distinguishing *four* facets in Dostoevsky's personality: the creative artist, the neurotic, the moralist and the sinner (ibid., p. 177). Freud maintains that the creative artist is the one that is least in doubt and places Dostoevsky not far behind Shakespeare, regarding his *The Brothers Karamazov* to be the "most magnificent novel ever written; the episode of the Grand Inquisitor, one of the peaks in the literature of the world ... Before the problem of the creative artist analysis must, alas, lay down its arms" (ibid.). In relation to the moral aspect of his character, Freud maintains that the moral man is he who, when he feels temptation in his heart, resists yielding to it. For Freud, the essence of morality lies in renunciation. As such, he regards Dostoevsky, who strived hard morally, to have failed. Freud proceeds to consider the criminal elements of Dostoevsky's rich personality structure. There are two character traits that Freud considers to be essential to the (common) criminal, and he found these to be likewise encountered in Dostoevsky: "boundless egoism and a strong destructive urge. Common to both of these, and a necessary condition for their expression, is absence of love, lack of an emotional appreciation of (human) objects" (ibid. p. 178). In a seeming paradox Freud states that although Dostoevsky possessed a great capacity for love and a great need to be loved, Freud nonetheless places him among the criminals. Why is this so?

> The answer is that it comes from his choice of material, which singles out from all others violent, murderous and egoistic characters, thus pointing to the existence of similar tendencies within himself, and also from certain facts in his life, like his passion for gambling and his possible confession to a sexual assault upon a young girl. The contradiction is resolved by the realisation that Dostoevsky's very strong destructive instinct, which might easily have made him a criminal, was in actual life directed mainly against his own person (inward instead of outward) and thus found expression in masochism and a sense of guilt. Nevertheless, his personality retained sadistic traits in plenty, which showed themselves in his irritability, his love of tormenting and his intolerance even towards people he loved, and which appear also in the way in which, as an author, he treats his readers. Thus in little things he was a sadist towards others, and in bigger things a sadist towards himself, in fact a masochist—that is to say the mildest, kindliest, most helpful person possible [ibid. pp. 178–179].

Freud divines *three* further factors in Dostoevsky's structure: his intense emotional life, his perverse, innate instinctual disposition "which marked him out to be a sado–masochist or a criminal" (ibid. p. 179), and his unanalyzable artistic gifts. Let us remark on the first two characterological traits. In his 18th year Dostoevsky's father was murdered and for most of his adult life Dostoevsky was afraid of death, suffering many death-like attacks which commentators have labelled "epilepsy", but which Freud defines as hysteria. What was the meaning of these death-like attacks? According to Freud, they signify an identification with a dead person or with somebody one wishes were dead. In the latter case, the attack has the value of a punishment. As Freud puts it: "One has wished another person dead, and now one *is* this other person and is dead oneself" (ibid. p. 183). According to psychoanalysis, the person one wishes dead, if one is male, is the father and the hysterical attack is then a self-punishment for a death wish against a despised and hated father. Patricide, as the primal crime of humanity (phylogenetically) and in the Oedipal phantasies of the individual (ontogenetically), is the main source of the sense of guilt, a fact repeated by Freud throughout all his works. And here again we see Freud relating crime to the Oedipus complex in which the male Oedipal child is ambivalently related to father in hate and love. In order to resolve his Oedipus complex at least partially, he must come to realise that because he is not the object of his mother's desire and that his father is, he has to relinquish his love for his mother. What he must do instead is identify with his father, who is the rival for his mother's affections and is therefore perceived as the aggressor. He realises, in other words, that the attempt to remove his father would be punished with castration and so, from fear of castration, he relinquishes his wish to marry his mother (incest) and murder his father (patricide). This wish, however, remains in the unconscious and forms the basis of the sense of guilt. If the father was cruel then the superego, as inheritor of parental influence, will also be cruel. In such cases, the superego becomes severe and sadistic while the ego is masochistic. A need for punishment then develops in the ego that will find satisfaction in the ill treatment meted out to it by the superego. As Freud states: "For every punishment is ultimately castration and, as such, a fulfilment of the old passive attitude towards the father. Even Fate is, in the last resort, only a later projection of the father" (ibid. p. 185). Such are the psychological processes involved in the formation of conscience.

According to Freud, Dostoevsky never succeeded in freeing himself from these feelings of guilt arising from his desire to murder his father. Dostoevsky's sympathy for criminals is based on an identification with similar murderous impulses in himself, according to Freud.

In this paper Freud also mentions *three* types of criminal: the common criminal whose motives are egotistical, the political and religious criminal (one could call him the person of desire), and the primal criminal (the one in all of us; the one excluded from sexual intercourse with the parents in the primal scene).

Sadism and guilt

In *Civilization and Its Discontents* (1930), Freud further explored the role of sadism. In his earlier theory of the instincts, Freud postulated the ego or self-preservative instincts on the one hand and the object or sexual instincts on the other hand. These latter libidinal instincts of love include the sadistic instinct—sadism regarded by Freud as being a part of sexual life. However, the later Freud postulated an independent, innate, aggressive instinct, which he discussed in greater detail in chapter vii and viii of this work. In this later modified theory of the instincts, the sexual and self-preservative instincts are subsumed by the life instincts (Eros), which are locked in immortal combat with the destructive death instincts (Thanatos). He felt the need to postulate such a death drive due to the ubiquity of nonerotic destructiveness and aggressivity.

> The inclination to aggression is an original, self-subsisting instinctual disposition in man, and ... it constitutes the greatest impediment to civilization ... man's natural aggressive instinct, the hostility of each against all and of all against each, opposes this programme of civilization [ibid. p. 59].

However, that said, sadism (the death drive) is entwined with the erotic aim. The struggle between Eros and Thanatos, between life and death, love and hate, works itself out in the human species. "This struggle is what all life essentially consists of, and the evolution of civilization may therefore be simply described as the struggle for life of the human species. And it is this battle of the giants that our nurse-maids try to appease with their lullaby about Heaven" (ibid.).

In part seven, Freud explicitly relates this death drive to the sense of guilt and the need for punishment. According to Freud, the human subject renders his desire for aggression innocuous by introjecting (internalising) it so that it is directed to his own ego where it is taken over by the superego, the critical agency within the ego, which watches over the ego like "a garrison in a conquered city" (ibid. p. 61). The ego is then subject to the same aggressiveness that it would itself have liked to satisfy on other subjects. The tension provoked by the conflict between ego and superego produces the sense of guilt and expresses itself as a need for punishment (ibid. p. 60; see also Freud, 1933, pp. 57–80). When authority becomes internalised through the establishment of the superego, the superego will torment or torture the "sinful" ego with anxiety and "is on the watch for opportunities of getting it punished by the external world" (Freud, 1928, p. 62). There are thus *two* origins of the sense of guilt: one that arises from fear of authority and the second one, which later on arises from fear of the superego. Where the first will insist on a renunciation of instinctual satisfactions, the second one will press for punishment. As Freud puts it:

> First comes renunciation of instinct owing to fear of aggression by the *external* authority. (This is, of course, what fear of the loss of love amounts to, for love is a protection against this punitive aggression.) After that comes the erection of an *internal* authority, and renunciation of instinct owing to fear of it—owing to fear of conscience. In the second situation bad intentions are equated with bad actions and hence comes a sense of guilt and a need for punishment [ibid. p. 65].

Freud notes that the severity of the superego, which a child develops, does not necessarily correspond to the severity of treatment he has experienced at the hands of his parents. A child who has been brought up very leniently can acquire a very strict superego. Innate constitutional and environmental factors are both important. This fact has been emphasised especially by Melanie Klein and her followers. In a footnote to this work Freud clarifies the situation and connects it with young criminals when he states:

> In delinquent children, who have been brought up without love, the tension between ego and super-ego is lacking, and the whole of their aggressiveness can be directed outwards. Apart from

constitutional factors which may be supposed to be present, it can be said, therefore, that a severe conscience arises from the joint operation of two factors: the frustration of instinct, which unleashes aggressiveness, and the experience of being loved, which turns the aggressiveness inwards and hands it over to the super-ego [ibid. p. 67].

In this chapter, Freud reiterates that the sense of guilt springs from the Oedipus complex and is acquired through the killing of the father by the band of brothers (ibid., p. 68). He distinguishes between *guilt* and *remorse*: when one has a sense of guilt after committing a misdeed and because of it, the feeling should be called *remorse*. It presupposes the readiness to feel guilt was already in existence prior to the deed (ibid., p. 74). Remorse is the result of primordial and primitive ambivalence of feeling towards the father, and since the inclination to aggression is repeated in succeeding generations, the sense of guilt will also persist, being an expression of the conflict (due to ambivalence) of the eternal struggle between the two Heavenly Powers, Eros and Thanatos (ibid., p. 69). As Goethe's *Wilhelm Meister* expresses it: "To earth, this weary earth, ye bring us/ To guilt ye let us heedless go,/ Then leave repentance fierce to wring us:/ A moment's guilt, an age of woe!" This conflict between love and hatred, between life and death is what all life essentially consists of according to Freud, and it plays itself out, not only ontogenetically in the individual, but also phylogenetically in the evolution of our species. It is enough to determine one's destiny as a neurotic, a pervert or a psychotic, in one of whose structures, bar the psychotic one, that the pale criminal will inevitably find himself inscribed as subject.

CHAPTER TWO

Jung: the spell of the shadow

"On a chair lay a razor, besmeared with blood. On the hearth were two or three long and thick tresses of grey human hair, also dabbled in blood, and seeming to have been pulled out by the roots ... a search was made in the chimney, and (horrible to relate!) the corpse of the daughter, head downward, was dragged therefrom ... Upon the fire were many severe scratches and, upon the throat, dark bruises, and deep indentations of finger nails, as if the deceased had been throttled to death ... the party made its way into a small paved yard in the rear of the building, where lay the corpse of the old lady, with her throat so entirely cut that, upon an attempt to raise her, the head fell off. The body, as well as the head, was fearfully mutilated—the former so much so as scarcely to retain any semblance of humanity"

Edgar Allan Poe, *The Murders in the Rue Morgue*

Carl Gustav Jung (1875–1961) pioneered "analytical psychology", thus differentiating his psychology from its Freudian counterpart. Nowhere in Jung's writings is there a systematic treatment of pale criminality, but he does mention criminals in relation to his early word association tests, and he addresses the issue of the pale and rosy criminal in his seminar on Nietzsche's *Thus Spake Zarathustra*, which I will examine. His conceptualisations on the *shadow* are directly relevant here and will also be explored in some detail. Before doing so, however, it seems appropriate to delineate some central Jungian concepts, as they will recur in our analysis of the contribution of analytical psychology to criminality. These comments serve also as a succinct introduction to Jungian psychology.

Central Jungian concepts

Central to Jung's contribution to the psychology of personality development is the concept of *individuation*. I shall adumbrate this concept and show how it relates to Jung's theories of the *Self*, the *ego* and the *archetypes* of the *collective unconscious*.

According to Jung, there is within the psyche an innate, inherited instinct teleologically tending towards wholeness, whose goal is the unification and integration of all aspects of the personality. Jung called this the process of individuation. It includes all psychological and mental processes, physiology and biology, positive and negative, realised and unrealised potentials and also a spiritual dimension. Individuation is the coming into being, or becoming of the Self. In Aristotelian teleological terms, it is the transition from potency to act.

For Jung, the ego is a complex of consciousness, the organ of perception, which delineates that of which we are conscious and locates us spacio–temporally. The ego is the executive of the personality, the agent of the reality principle. The ego may be an entity at the centre of consciousness but, according to Jung, it cannot be regarded as the centre of the psyche, as it was for Freud. Jung postulated the Self as the centre of the totality of the psyche. The Self pursues purpose and yearns for meaning. The ego arises out of, and is subordinate to, the Self. Jung observes:

> The ego stands to the self as the moved to the mover, or as object to subject, because the determining factors which radiate from the self surround the ego on all sides and are therefore supraordinate to it.

The self, like the unconscious, is an *a priori* existent out of which the ego evolves [*CW* 11, para. 391].

The Self is the central archetype, the archetype of all archetypes. Archetypes are nonrepresentable structuring patterns of psychological performance linked to the instincts, which order experience. Jung first introduced the word in 1919 and acknowledged philosophical precedents such as Plato, with his theory of the Forms or Ideas, Kant, with his notion of the *a priori* form, and Schopenhauer with his account of "prototypes". Whereas the "personal unconscious" is our ontogenetic inheritance and comprises the complexes, the "collective unconscious" is our phylogenetic inheritance comprising the archetypes. Jung discovered that similar motifs occurred in different cultures corresponding to "nodal points" within the psyche. The archetype, as a basic predisposition acquired during evolution, becomes conscious as its form is actualised in outer experience. Archetypes are connected to the developmental stages in life. "Frustration of archetypal intent" can occur when there are no initiatory stages or ceremonies giving rise to the syndrome of, in the case of a man, the *puer aeternus* (the eternal boy). Jung distinguished between the archetype *per se*, which is the innate releasing mechanism responsible for patterns of experience and the archetypal *image*, which is the outer experience that matches the inner potential for development.

The special function of the Self is to balance and pattern all the other archetypes as well as all of a person's life in terms of its potential purpose. Jung noted that there was a tendency for the archetypes to personify. He listed a number of them. The *persona* (the mask actors wore) is the mediator between the ego and the external world (i.e., one's social roles). The ego can become identified with the persona, with a job or a role and this can cause difficulties. It is usually the first archetype to be worked with in Jungian analysis as it is the most accessible of all, the one closest to consciousness. The *shadow*, which we will discuss in greater detail when we come to considering its relationship with criminality, is the unconscious part of the personality, characterised by traits and tendencies, positive or negative, that the ego either ignores or rejects. Frequently, we meet the shadow (projections) in other people. The *animus* (*logos*) is the contrasexual complex in the woman whereas the *anima* (*eros*) is the contrasexual complex in the man. In other words, the animus is the masculine principle in a woman and the anima is the feminine principle in a man. They connect us with inner figures, outer figures as well as with the creative unconscious. Other archetypes include the Great Mother, the Wise Old Man etc. The Self embraces ego-consciousness, the shadow, the anima, animus and the collective unconscious. The Self functions as a synthesiser of opposites within the psyche which include: ego/self, conscious/unconscious, personal/collective, extraversion/introversion anima/animus, Eros/Logos, image/instinct etc. This psychological oppositionalism in Jungian psychology shows affinity with the Hegelian dialectics of thesis, antithesis, and synthesis—Jung's transcendent function.

There is also opposition present in Jungian typology. In 1921, after his break with Freud, Jung developed his theory of *psychological types*. According to Jung, there are *two* attitudes and *four* functions of consciousness. *Extraversion* and *introversion* are the two attitudes. The extravert is energised by the external world, the introvert by the internal one. Jung acknowledged that no one was a pure extravert or introvert. The four functions of consciousness are: *thinking, feeling, sensation* and *intuition*. The two *rational* functions comprise thinking (logical thought) and feeling (evaluation) while the two *nonrational* functions include sensation (sensing reality) and intuition (perceiving the potential of things). The *superior* function is the most well adapted function while the *inferior* function is the least adapted one. For example, if one were a thinking type, feeling would be the inferior function. As thinking and feeling are opposites, so too are sensation and intuition. Understanding someone's typology has practical implications. To a large extent, individuation involves coming to terms with one's opposite in the unconscious and is promoted in Jungian analysis. The goal is, to quote Jung, "to attain a conscious attitude which allows the unconscious to co-operate instead of being drawn into opposition" (*CW* 16, para. 366). Hopefully, the result will be harmony between the unconscious and consciousness.

While the ego is directed towards the *emergence from* the unconscious, the Self is oriented towards *union with* the unconscious. It is an ordering and unifying principle, which directs the course of psychological development. It does this by producing numinous symbols of a self-regulatory nature. *Self-regulation* is a balancing, a *compensation*, that is to say, a rectification of a previously unbalanced attitude. For Jung, the psyche is self-regulatory; it is the psychical equivalent of physical homeostasis. For example, mania could be a myopic, maladaptive defence against depression. A neurosis can be seen as a rift or rupture between consciousness and the unconscious, clinically showing through the various ego defences of "splitting", "projection", "introjection", "projective identification", "intellectualism" etc. In analytic praxis, by unearthing and uncovering what lurks behind the ego defences, psychic energy can be released. In restructuring the conscious position, psychic equilibrium can be restored.

In stating this, Jung is holding a purposive and prospective view of the neuroses in contradistinction to Freud's retrospective viewpoint. In the individuation process, the transition is from instinct to symbols and transcendence. Whereas in Freudian psychoanalysis symbols are primarily defensive, in Jung's view, they are purposive and healing. In short, the Self symbolises the infinitude of the archetype and points paradigmatically to a meaning that is beyond description and conceptualisation. As such, a symbol is not a sign. Symbols work towards self-regulation and are ciphers of spirituality showing traces of transcendence because symbols work in the service of the Self. Symbols of wholeness are epitomised or exemplified by *mandalas* (a Sanskrit word meaning "magical circle"), said by Jung to express the totality of the psyche and the centre of the personality, the Self radiated and revealed as a transpersonal entity.

The Self reconciles opposites, the bipolarity inherent in all psychic functioning. This reconciliation of opposites occupies much of the process of integration and individuation. The Self, which has no parallel in Freudian psychoanalysis, is at once an archetypal image of man's fullest potential, the unification of the personality and the reconciliation of the opposites. Indeed, the synthesis of the opposites is crucial to the integration of the personality and to a sense of wholeness. The unconscious will activate what Jung refers to as the *transcendent function*, which he defines as "a natural process, a manifestation of the energy that springs from the tension of the opposites and it consists in a series of fantasy occurrences which appear spontaneously in dreams and visions" (*CW* 7, para.

121). The transcendent function mediates opposites, expressing itself by way of symbols and facilitating the transition from one psychological attitude to another. Individuation can be seen as a *circumambulation* of the Self, in other words, a circular movement as well as the marking of a sacred precinct around a central point. *Circumambulation* was an alchemical term used for a concentration upon the centre of creative change. The "circle" is a metaphor for the containment necessary during analysis in order to withstand the tensions produced by the meeting of opposites and to prevent psychic disruption and disintegration. Clinically, circumambulation is a working-through of the *complexes*, which are groups of related images having a common emotional tone gathered or grouped around an archetypal core and which Jung regarded as the *via regia* to the unconscious.

The realising or actualising of one's unique Self is the goal of a lifetime. Individuation involves a differentiation and separation from the collective. The practice and process of analysis deals with the constant dialectical interplay between ego and Self. It attempts to activate the inborn, innate instinct to individuate, which involves the shift of psychic balance from the area of consciousness with the ego at its centre, to the totality of both conscious and unconscious psyche. Individuation is thus a *natural* tendency and it does not occur in isolation; it takes place in *sociality* rather than *solitude*. Jung exhorts us to pay attention to our dreams, to engage in *active imagination* (or directed day-dreaming) and to delve down into our depths in order to understand ourselves more fully and creatively. His injunction is that we realise ourselves completely, that is to say, that we individuate. This is a task of universal importance because the instinct and natural inclination to individuate is ubiquitous, relevant for all peoples everywhere, because the Self is the seed of our innermost being. The central Jungian concept is, arguably, that of the archetype, which we will now look at in detail.

Archetypes

According to the Jungians, the human subject is equipped with a vast, perhaps limitless, number of archetypal imperatives, and frustration of this archetypal programme can result in psychopathology. Jung conceived of archetypes as biological entities. As Jung stated, the archetype:

> is not meant to denote an inherited idea, but rather an inherited mode of functioning, corresponding to the inborn way in which the chick emerges from the egg, the bird builds its nest, a certain kind of wasp stings the motor ganglion of the caterpillar, and eels find their way to the Bermudas. In other words, it is a 'pattern of behaviour'. This aspect of the archetype, the purely biological one, is the proper concern of scientific psychology [CW 18, para. 1228].

In what follows, particular attention will be paid to the archetype of the family because it is from a dehiscence in the family that much pathology emerges, a fact recognised by all the analytical schools. The Jungian archetype is, as we have said, a biological entity, a "living organism, endowed with generative force" (CW 6, para. 6 n. 9). Archetypes are innate predispositions that transcend culture, race and time. They are determined by our ontogenesis (personal history) and our phylogenesis (collective history). They are biologically encoded in our brains and behaviour and have evolved over time. They represent our phylogenetic blueprint with which all of us are endowed. Because we possess the same brain and bodily structure, we function similarly. If our common biology is inherited, the archetypes must also be similar and inherited too. Examples of archetypal manifestations include the following: the experience of being born, being mothered, exploring our environment, playing with peers, infancy, childhood, adolescence, being initiated, establishing a place in society, finding a partner, marrying and child-rearing for most, loving, fighting, participating in religious ritual, social responsibilities, middle age, senescence and preparation for death. As Jung wrote: "Ultimately, every individual is the same as the eternal life of the species" (CW 11, para. 146). Archetype was a term introduced by Jung in 1919 (see CW 8, para. 270) to denote a "prime imprinter" or "imprimatur", correspond to "nodal points" or typical dispositions within the structure of the psyche.

The archetypal form or pattern is inherited but the content is changeable and variable. From 1946 onwards, Jung distinguished between the archetype *as such*, the archetype *qua* archetype, which is an unknowable nucleus that "never was conscious and never will be" (*CW* 9i, para. 266) and the archetypal image. Jung is adamant:

> the archetypal representation (images or ideas) mediated to us by
> the unconscious should not be confused with the archetype as such.
> They are very varied ... and point back to one essential
> 'unrepresentable' basic form. The latter is characterised by certain
> formal elements and by certain fundamental meanings, although
> these can only be grasped approximately" [*CW* 8, para. 417].

For Jung, archetypes are "biological norms of psychic activity" (*CW*
9i, para. 309n). Such experiences of life and the emotions to which
they give rise form a structural psychical residue. Repeated
experiences leave these residual psychic structures, which evolve
to become archetypal structures and pre-existing patterns. The
baby, for example, does not *learn* how to breathe and excrete. This is
an innate psychological schema. Jung observes: "the collective
unconscious is an image of the world that has taken aeons to form.
In this image certain features, the archetypes or dominants, have
crystallised out in the course of time. They are the ruling powers"
(*CW* 7, para. 151). The baby's experience is structured by innate
archetypal forms. It is this interaction and exchange between such
innate structures on the one hand, and early environmental
experiences on the other hand, that plays a crucial role in the
healthy or pathological development of the subject. The archetype
is, as Jung describes it, "a system of readiness for action" (*CW* 9i,
para. 199).

Jung connects the archetypes to the instincts. In the earlier Jung,
what an archetype is to psychology, the instinct is to biology. Jung
notes: "the collective unconscious consists of the sum of the instincts
and their correlates, the archetypes" (*CW* 8, para. 338). Later on,
Jung dissolved the distinction between psychology and biology,
maintaining that it was a false division and misleading dichotomy.
Archetypes, as conceived by the later Jung, are essentially
psychosomatic entities occupying a place between instinct and
image. Archetypes incorporate biology, the drives (the instincts)
and are connected to the spirit and the creative imagination (the
image). They are dual, bipolar and bifurcated in nature. Jung thus
links psychology, biology (and ethology) and the spirit. His is an
undus mundus, the Presocratic One in the Many.

In 1947, Jung introduced the term *psychoid unconscious* to

describe an area of the psyche so deep and buried that it does not derive from man's biological or neurological base. The psychoid unconscious "cannot be directly perceived or "represented"" (CW 8, para. 417). It does not reach consciousness.

Archetypes have parallels in the philosophies of Plato, Kant and Schopenhauer, with ethology, (socio)biology, neurology, mythology and structuralist linguistics (Chomsky), and has found ample scientific corroboration. Jung himself drew parallels between archetypes and animal behaviour.

> Let us take as an example the incredibly refined instinct of propagation of the yucca moth. The flowers of the yucca plant open for one night only. The moth takes the pollen from one of the flowers and kneads it into a little pellet. Then it visits a second flower, cuts open the pistil, lays its eggs between the ovules and then stuffs the pellet into the funnel-shaped opening of the pistil. Only once in its life does it carry out this operation ... the yucca moth must carry within it an image, as it were, of the situation that 'triggers off' its instinct. This image enables it to 'recognise' the yucca flower and its structure [CW 8, paras. 268 and 277].

Numerous analytical psychologists have linked modern ethology with archetypal theory. Fordham (1957) considers Tinbergen's conception of innate releasing mechanisms (IRMs) in animals as being applicable to the archetypal programmes of humans. Jacobi (1959) connects Lorenz's "innate schemata" with archetypes. Storr (1973) relates IRMs to the innate archetypal predispositions with which infants are born. And Stevens, in his *Archetype: A Natural History of the Self* (1982), to which I am here indebted, draws heavily on ethology, sociobiology and archetypal theory, defining archetypes as "innate neuropsychic centres" (p. 296). In terms of biology, Stevens suggests that it is in the DNA itself that we must look for the location and transmission of archetypes. For Stevens, DNA is "the replicable archetype of the species" (p. 73). In terms of neurology, Rossi (1977) suggests that archetypes are located in the right cerebral hemisphere of the brain. This work has been extended by the neurophysiologist Henry (1977). In structuralist linguistics, Noam Chomsky refers to "universals" and unifying structures or patterns of language acquisition in children. Piaget writes of innate "schemata", which underpin percepto-motor activity. In anthropology, Lévi-Strauss concluded that present collective phenomena represent transformation of earlier infra-structures. Finally, Andrew Samuels (1985) shows some parallels with psychoanalysis in the work of Lacan, Bion and Klein. He maintains that Lacan's Symbolic order, which structures the unconscious through laws and language, may be aligned with Jung's theory of archetypes. Yes, but there is this difference in my opinion: for Lacan, man is caught up in an *exogenous* structural order (the Symbolic), whereas for Jung, man is caught in an *endogenous* network of archetypal order. He links, I think somewhat misleadingly, Lacan's Imaginary with Jung's personal unconscious, but I concur with him that Lacan's concept of the Real approaches Jung's elaboration of the "psychoid unconscious". In relation to Bion, Samuels connects Bion's notion of "proto-thoughts" (thoughts which precede a thinking capacity) and which become "preconceptions" with archetypes in that preconceptions are predisposing psychosomatic entities. Lastly, in relation to Klein, Samuels opines that Klein's notion of "unconscious phantasy" is the psychoanalytic idea that is most clearly aligned with archetypal theory.

Archetypes are, thus, innate psychic structures of the phyloge-netic psyche. As Jung states: "the collective unconscious contains the whole spiritual heritage of mankind's evolution, born anew in the brain structure of every individual" (*CW* 8, para. 342). The process of this archetypal actualisation Jung labelled *individuation*. He observes: "Individuation is an expression of that biological process—simple or complicated as the case may be—by which every living thing becomes what it was destined to become from the beginning" (*CW* 11, para. 144).

Criminals and the word association tests

Let me mention Jung's very early work with word association tests and how they relate to criminality before going on to deal with Jung's seminar on Nietzsche's *Zarathustra* and adumbrating his conceptualisations on the shadow. In relation to word association tests, Jung writes: "I use this test now not with patients but with criminal cases" (*CW* 18, para. 97). In these experiments, a hundred words or so are given. The test person is instructed to react with the first word that comes immediately to mind after hearing the stimulus word. The time of each reaction is recorded. After the experiment another one is carried out. The stimulus words are repeated and the test person has to reproduce his former answer. In certain places his memory fails and mistakes are made, all of which are important, especially if the reaction time is delayed. A particular word, such as "knife" or "kill", especially when used in a word experiment with someone suspected of murder, can uncover a complex, that is to say, a conglomeration of psychic contents characterised by a painful feeling–tone. Complexes are laden with affect. In this way, something hidden from sight sees the daylight. The prolongation of the reaction time is extremely important, as are reactions with more than one word, or reactions expressed by facial gestures, laughing, coughing, stammering, movement of the hands, feet or body, or reactions like "yes" and "no". Jung observes: "If you put it to a criminal he can refuse, and that is fatal because one knows why he refuses. If he gives in he hangs himself. In Zurich I am called in by the Court when they have a difficult case; I am the last straw" (ibid. para. 102).

Jung frequently gave evidence early in his career as a psychiatrist using the word association test. Through his word association experiment, Jung succeeded in revealing a number of crimes the people in question committed. He maintained that the application of the experiment to the delinquent lies in the exploration of the complex underlying the crime (see CW 2, para. 755). In a number of cases, the culprits confessed to their crimes (mostly of theft) arising from the association experiment. (See ibid. pp. 439–465 where Jung unmasked a culprit in a crime of theft and reminds us that Christ was in the place of the criminal).

Jung realised that his word-association experiment does not provide absolute proof of guilt but a valuable addition to the circumstantial evidence (see ibid. para. 1330). Jung asserts that sometimes it is difficult to distinguish between the guilty and the innocent, presumably because the so-called innocents have committed some misdeeds, so much so that Jung enquires: "Why do the innocent usually show signs of a guilt-complex?" (ibid. para. 1332).

The soul of the criminal

In "Crime and the Soul" (CW 18), Jung suggests that the criminal possesses a dual personality in that, generally speaking, the criminal yearns to be respectable. Indeed, large numbers of criminals lead middle-class existences and commit their crimes "through their second selves" (ibid. para. 800). Jung describes how a man can, in Lacanian terminology, suddenly fall from the Symbolic into the Real. "It is a terrible fact that crime seems to creep up on the criminal as something foreign that gradually gains a hold on him so that eventually he has no knowledge from one moment to another what he is about to do" (ibid. para. 801). He gives an example of a 9-year-old boy who one day stabbed his sister with scissors: from boyhood to budding criminality. Later, this boy became epileptic which, for Jung, represented, in this case, an evasion of the crime, a repression of the criminal instinct. Jung notes: "Unconsciously people try to escape the inner urge to crime by taking refuge in illness" (ibid. para. 815).

Illness is one defence mechanism, we can say. Another way of mitigating the full force of the crimes one would like to commit but would never dare, is to transmit the criminal instincts to others and have them carry out the deeds, by proxy as it were. Jung gives the example of a man who killed his family and dog, stabbing his wife 11 times. His wife, who was a fanatical member of a fundamentalist religious sect, unconsciously transmitted the evil in her to her husband, Jung maintains. She had persuaded him that he was evil and that she was all good and "instilled the criminal instinct into his subconscious mind. It was characteristic that the husband recited a saying from the Bible at each stab, which best indicates the origin of his hostility" (ibid. para. 818).

Jung shares with the psychoanalytic theorists the view that we are all repressed criminals and that the dividing line between the criminal and the noncriminal is not strictly demarcated. He observes:

> Far more crime, cruelty, and horror occur in the human soul than in the external world. The soul of the criminal, as manifested in his deeds, often affords an insight into the deepest psychological processes of humanity in general. Sometimes it is quite remarkable

what a background such murders have, and how people are driven to perpetrate acts which at any other time and of their own accord they would never commit [ibid. para. 819].

"We are all potential murderers", Jung states (*CW* 2, p. 453). He gives an example of a baker who murdered three people in a cataleptic state. His wife was a member of the same sect as the woman in the previous example. With regards to this unconscious transmission of criminal instinct, Jung writes:

> The more evil a person is, the more he tries to force upon others the wickedness he does not want to show to the outside world. The baker and the Rhinelander [the other criminal case] were respectable men. Before they committed their crimes they would have been amazed had anyone thought them capable of such things. They certainly never intended to commit murder. This idea was unconsciously instilled into them as a means of abreacting the evil instincts of their wives. Man is a very complicated thing, and though he knows a great deal about all sorts of things, he knows very little about himself [*CW* 18, para. 821].

In "The Undiscovered Self: Present and Future" (*CW* 10), Jung writes more about the evil lurking in the soul of man. According to Jung, the evil dwelling in the heart of man is of "gigantic proportions" (ibid. para. 571). He observes:

> The evil, the guilt, the profound unease of conscience, the dark foreboding, are there before our eyes, if only we would see. Man has done these things; I am a man, who has his share of human nature; therefore I am guilty with the rest and bear unaltered and indelibly within me the capacity and the inclination to do them again at any time. Even if, juristically speaking, we were not accessories to the crime, we are always, thanks to our human nature, potential criminals. In reality we merely lacked a suitable opportunity to be drawn into the infernal mêlée. None of us stands outside humanity's black collective shadow. Whether the crime occurred many generations back or happens today it remains the symptom of a disposition that is always and everywhere present [ibid. para. 572].

For Jung then, evil is "lodged in human nature itself" (ibid. para. 573). It would seem that as well as being split, dual and dissociated, we are all potential criminals shoving our criminal shadow side onto others or the devil. As Jung notes: "We therefore prefer to localize the evil in individual criminals or groups of criminals while washing our hands in innocence and ignoring the general proclivity to evil" (ibid. para. 573). We stand like so many Pontious Pilates, the criminal's soul lurking within us all—lacking in love. And as Jung states: "Where love stops, power begins, and violence, and terror" (ibid. para. 580).

The criminal in Nietzsche's Zarathustra

Jung devoted the years 1934 to 1939 to elucidating, in seminars in Zurich, the psychological strands of Nietzsche's *Thus Spake Zarathustra*, in which Nietzsche discusses and distinguishes between the *pale and rosy* criminal. (Jung, 1934–1939). The pale criminal, as distinct from a rosy one, "does not feel well in his skin" (ibid. p. 452). Paleness in someone denotes that he looks unhealthy. According to Jung, a criminal, be he pale or rosy, shows by his crimes his desire to destroy himself. "He has committed murder so that he will be judged and his head will be cut off [referring to Nietzsche's text], and that is what he wanted. Moreover, when a person murders, he has murdered himself morally, which is of course just as bad as real death" (ibid., p. 453). This is the meaning of punishment—if a man murders we kill him. (Of course, Jung was writing at a time when capital punishment was much more widespread in the world than it is today). Furthermore, in murdering, the man has an advantage on us because "we have all wanted to do that" (ibid.). In fact, our ancestors have universally been murderers. It is, according to Jung, innate within us, in our blood. We refrain from murdering because we have civilised moral sanctions, though we do it collectively and call it "law". In this way we are satisfied. Everyone thus receives "his sprinkling of blood for his own salvation" (ibid. p. 453). "It gives people a fine feeling to have committed a certain amount of crime. That is the psychology of crime" (ibid. pp. 453–4).

Jung gives an example. In the Celebes it is the custom for the prisoner to be killed by the whole crowd, who stick their spears into the victim and lick his blood until eventually he dies. Everyone has a taste of his blood. It is a type of communion. Each member of the primitive tribe shares in the killing, thus establishing a connection through a common cannibalistic type ritual. Since we do not have that chance, we content ourselves with reading detective novels or going to the cinema to watch horror movies, Jung maintains (see ibid. p. 454). We are thus thrilled by accounts of crimes. Jung observes:

> The psychology of killing is the psychology of the criminal, so there are even murderers who want to be put to death and are not satisfied if they are not. In certain murderers there is a sacrificial psychology; they thus feel their importance over people. All that is in the death of Christ; he was counted as a criminal and crucified between two thieves and in place of a thief. He was exchanged against Barabbas who was freed ... So Christ was very much in the place of the criminal, he was the god of the past year that is crucified for the good of the community [ibid., p. 454].

To return to the pale criminal: the pale criminal is so named because he collapses at the idea of it; he is a man "who is not on the level of his deed" (ibid. p. 462). In writing *Zarathustra*, Nietzsche becomes an "intellectual criminal" (ibid. p. 459), flirting with misdeeds and madness, reaching out into forbidden land and confronting his own evil. After the chapter in Nietzsche's *Zarathustra* on "Delights and Passions" there is the chapter on "The Pale Criminal". For Jung it is not surprising, because if one follows the path of one's passion one inevitably comes to the place where one's passion becomes "abnormal, asocial or criminal, and this is a quality which is in everybody" (ibid. p. 463). One cannot, however, escape one's passions or one's sufferings (*passio* means suffering). So arriving at the pale criminal is perfectly normal, but the way in which we deal with the pale criminal is the test of mental soundness or otherwise. One must know what one does. Nietzsche's criminal, in committing his crimes, made himself a criminal because he was a criminal. But if he is a criminal without realising it, in simply committing his crime he has no chance of redemption. If he knows what he does there is a chance because he is fulfilling his role, according to Jung. If a good man performs a good deed, there is no "moral must" in it because he will feel miserable if he fails to carry it out. The good man does it naturally, unconsciously, instinctively.

Jung highlights the fact that we must be conscious of our role, of Karma (see ibid. p. 465). In Hinduism, the condition of redemption is dependent on being conscious of what one does. "And from that point of view it is just as bad to be good without knowing it as to be bad without knowing it: neither way has merit; the only chance for redemption is in consciousness" (ibid.). Nietzsche's pale criminal knows what he is doing. The "greed for the blood" in Nietzsche's murderer is simply the preparation for his death. He is seeking to end his existence. "So the Pale Criminal is in that respect the symbol for the man who must end his existence because he is no good—in order to make room for the Superman" (ibid). He commits moral suicide by becoming a superman, outside ordinary morals, beyond good and evil. If the criminal knows that he is committing his crime to kill himself, then he will commit his crime. One judges a crime differently if the murderer kills himself immediately afterwards. One feels that he has judged himself guilty and that is satisfactory (ibid. p. 466).

We all want to kill—"everyone of us contains a criminal who wants to commit crime though we don't know it" (ibid.). Our criminal instincts are roused and we must have our revenge. "We are really just waiting for the time when we can take a revolver and kill; we are waiting for an age of revolution, for an age of cruelty" (ibid.). The murderer has murdered himself long before we take his life. For Nietzsche, the criminal is a man astray, a moral outsider who, through the act of murder, has done an evil to himself (see ibid. p. 468). As Jung puts it: "every case I am treating has a criminal in himself. If one goes far enough, everybody has done something or is planning to do something which is not right, which is criminal" (ibid.). But Jung says that he cannot talk about the analysis of a murderer as they do not come to him for treatment and each case is individual. He will not even say that all murderers should be analysed. And in relation to one's own criminality, pale or otherwise, Jung asserts that one must see one's criminal point, the criminal personality in oneself. Until then, one cannot become integrated. "The purpose of individuation is that every part of the individual must be integrated, also the criminal part; otherwise it is left by itself and works evil" (ibid. p. 469). This means accepting the shadow and assimilating it to consciousness; then one can do something about it, not to judge it or to moralise. As Jung states:

"We can improve when we accept what is part of ourselves. Then we can change, not before" (ibid.). We will be returning to this point shortly.

The paleness of the pale criminal is due to the fact the criminal was made pale by an idea; he begins to think about what he has done and to name it. He is unable to tolerate the vision of himself as criminal, unlike the rosy criminal who celebrates the fact of his own criminal character. When he says to himself that he has committed murder and sees it in the newspapers in print, he then realises that he has done this dreadful deed called murder. According to Jung, most murderers say: "I put a knife into him" or "I had to shoot him". Only later, the fact that it is actually murder dawns on him. Then they realise it and grow pale. Jung says that people who commit a fraud are astonished to find out that it carries such an ugly name as *crime*! The pale criminal, as Jung puts it, is slain by his own idea. That is the Jungian exploration of the *paleness* of the pale criminal.

Nietzsche goes on to address the cause of the crime. Murder is always a by-product. It is not performed for a certain purpose. Murderers are always astonished when it works. But in the unconscious, as Nietzsche conceives it, it is really murder—thirst for blood. The murderer, however, prefers the explanation that it was for robbery, for example. For Nietzsche, at least as Jung reads him, the criminal is a mass of diseases, a coil of serpents. He is pained and tortured and commits a crime. Jung philosophises that no-one causes pain to another unless he himself has experienced pain. Those who hurt and torture are those who have been hurt and tortured. They want to achieve their own suffering by hurting others. It is as if we want someone else (anybody else) to commit a crime so that we can say: "*There* is the criminal. *There* is the evil" (ibid. p. 471). That is why, Jung conjectures, we love detective novels or reports of crimes in the newspapers; "they fascinate us because we have an unsatisfied criminal instinct in ourselves" (ibid.).

A murderer, Jung opines, is a scapegoat for the community. Christ was the "murderer of the season" (ibid. p. 472). But Barabbas was the real criminal. Through Christ's death we are redeemed from sin. "When the community puts the criminal to death, it is an act of redemption for the community, a sort of psychological alleviation" (ibid.). The criminal has a social role and so he is accorded the dignity of a ritual in recognition of his merit—a trial with judges and barristers in wigs and gowns, a procession to the gallows, soldiers, a great crowd, the stage where the execution will take place. The great social importance of the crime is the atonement for the sins of the people. Jung makes another interesting point: if we identify with virtue, for example faithfulness, then it will be the forerunner of crime, because to burden the scale of virtues means that the scale of vices rises. Jung clarifies thus: "The more people think that they are good or identify with good, the more they leave evil alone, and as much as their good increases, unconsciously their evil will increase" (ibid. p. 473). So beware of the good person!

These views in Nietzsche, read by Jung, are potentially dangerous. That is why Jung cautions that no one should read Nietzsche's *Zarathustra* who has not been trained in the psychology of the unconscious. It is easy to misinterpret the work and to justify one's own evil by it. In fact, if read properly, it is, according to Jung, an incredibly moral book (see ibid. pp. 475–6).

Nietzsche is concerned with the evil of mankind, with universal humanity as it is represented in himself. So Jung says that he is concerned with the collective unconscious (see ibid. p. 480). He notes that, "the Pale Criminal is a form in the collective unconscious, the criminal in everybody" (ibid.). On the conscious level, everyone knows what a criminal is, but from the level below the threshold of consciousness, the criminal is no longer a statistic or a social or juristic phenomenon, but a symbolic or psychological concept, "a concept of the twilight, in the region of the pénombre where things have two sides, the sun side and the moon side" (ibid. p. 481). The sun leads from above, the moon from below. It is thus a twilight concept and only people "who have experienced the shadow can really understand what he [Nietzsche] is talking about" (ibid.). If people read Nietzsche at the level of consciousness, they not only misread but grossly misinterpret him as well, and will become horrified at what they read. The two levels, consciousness and the unconscious, (both the personal and the collective) must not be confused. And, for Jung, Nietzsche is speaking from the level of the collective unconscious in that he is talking of the crimes of men, every man. Jung observes: "Whoever is on the level of the personal unconscious has still a sort of luminosity on top from the sun, but down below it is all moonshine: treacherous, poisonous, evil, not to be trusted" (ibid. p. 482). The chapter on the pale criminal should not, Jung feels, be told in the daylight but at night under the seal of secrecy. The opposite of the values of consciousness is absolute shadow. And what on the surface is said to be criminal (perhaps it was criminal of Nietzsche to write such a work?), is a truth five thousand feet down, "a truth of the darkness", as Jung labels it (ibid. p. 483). In *Zarathustra*, Nietzsche was somewhere in the collective part of his unconscious, Jung surmises. In contradistinction, Nietzsche's *Genealogy of Morals* and his aphorisms would be more from the personal unconscious, Jung maintains.

A pale criminal is someone who, for Jung, commits a crime expecting to get caught, to be punished and to undergo suffering. That is why he commits the crime (ibid. p. 484). It would seem, here, that Jung is in full agreement with Freud. Just as a good man is he who has done the right thing, expecting recognition or reward. Good must be rewarded and evil punished, Jung maintains. What, though, of a crime that turns out to be a good thing? It is possible, admits Jung, but it does not stop us from considering it a crime and punishing it. As regards punishment, it must be according to the nature of the criminal. If we could produce criminals with a moral sense we could arrest them and give them a good talking to, knowing that their promises not to re-offend would be trustworthy. Likewise, if someone commits a crime in the heat of the moment, then Jung agrees that punishment can be postponed, but if he re-offends the whole severity of the law should come down upon him. To improve the lot of the prisoner is sentimental, according to Jung, because prisoners do not improve. "The real criminal makes fun of this leniency in punishment" (ibid. p. 487). It is as cruel to kill as it is to condemn to imprisonment for 25 years. Jung says if he had a choice he would prefer to die (ibid. p. 488). Every offender has the right to be punished, "and if we are too human or reasonable about it, we deprive him of the punishment he naturally expects" (ibid. p. 764). Furthermore, punishment ought not to be administered for the moral improvement of the culprit or for purposes of prevention, but because he has given offence (see ibid. p. 764). Punishment is precisely a feeling retaliation.

The criminal represents a protest against any and every social correction and relationship. The pale criminal is pale because he realises he is alone, outside society, an outcast. Jung states:

> The criminal is quite certainly asocial, disrupts the laws of humanity, and sins against all the rules of the human community; whoever commits a crime is cut off. He has to keep his crime secret, upsets the feeling of his fellow beings, violates their rights: he is the most violent breaker of the bond of human community [ibid. p. 489].

Jung informs us that once he had a pale criminal (viz., one unable to be a criminal) in his consulting room—a murderess. She could not stand the isolation the secret caused. Nietzsche realised the pale criminal in himself. Such a man cannot abide the eremitical isolation. Nietzsche's and Jung's exhortation: "Realise yourself, even and including your criminality".

With regards to judgement, Jung has this to say: "The more you know about the psychology of crime the less you can judge it; when you have seen many such cases, you just give up" (ibid. p. 1452). But, in giving up, you give up on your hatred and contempt, and on your revolt against evil and belief in the good, Jung admits. Practically, we have to pass judgement. When a criminal offends against the moral law (or moral laws) he becomes "a moral exile" (ibid. p. 1453), terminally haunted by the secret of his misdeeds. He cannot escape the judge in himself [the Freudian "superego", the Jungian "moral complex"] because the entire moral system is based upon archetypes of human behaviour.

So, the offender suffers when he commits an offence. In such criminal cases, sometimes one suffers from a corresponding disintegration of personality, perhaps amounting to a neurosis. The criminal really needs to be punished. "A man is dishonoured by the fact that he is not properly punished. His misdeed must be punished, must have compensation, or why in hell should he risk punishment?" (ibid.). Punishment may be his only reward. Moreover, many people commit sins simply in order to repent them (see ibid. p. 1454).

The shadow

On December 18th 1913, Jung had the following dream. He records it in his "autobiography" *Memories, Dreams, Reflections* (1961):

I was with an unknown, brown-skinned man, a savage, in a lonely, rocky mountain landscape. It was before dawn; the eastern sky was already bright, and the stars fading. Then I heard Siegfried's horn sounding over the mountains and I knew that we had to kill him. We were armed with rifles and lay in wait for him on a narrow path over the rocks. Then Siegfried appeared high up on the crest of the mountain, in the first ray of the rising sun. On a chariot made of the bones of the dead he drove at furious speed down the precipitous slope. When he turned a corner, we shot at him, and he plunged down, struck dead. Filled with disgust and remorse for having destroyed something so great and beautiful, I turned to flee, impelled by the fear that the murder might be discovered. But a tremendous downfall of rain began, and I knew that it would wipe out all traces of the dead. I had escaped the danger of discovery; life would go on, but an unbearable feeling of guilt remained [p. 204].

Jung interprets the small, brown-skinned savage who accompanied him and who had initiated the killing as an embodiment of the primitive shadow. We have already mentioned Jung's concept of the shadow and its relationship with criminality in passing. This concept will now be explored in much greater detail. In Jung's theorising, the shadow is the inferior part of the personality. It is the sum of all personal and collective psychic elements which, due to their incompatibility with the chosen conscious attitude, are denied expression and coalesce into a "splinter personality" which possesses relative autonomy. The shadow behaves as a compensation to consciousness; its effects being positive as well as negative. Jung describes it thus: "The shadow personifies everything that the subject refuses to acknowledge about himself and yet is always thrusting itself upon him directly or indirectly—for instance, inferior traits of character and other incompatible tendencies" (CW 9, p. 284). Elsewhere he describes it thus:

The shadow is that hidden, repressed, for the most part inferior and guilt-laden personality whose ultimate ramifications reach back into the realm of our animal ancestors and so comprise the whole historical aspect of the unconscious ... If it has been believed hitherto that the human shadow was the source of all evil, it can now be ascertained on closer investigation that the unconscious man, that is, his shadow, does not consist of morally reprehensible tendencies, but also displays a number of good qualities, such as moral instincts, appropriate reaction, realistic insights, creative impulses, etc. [ibid. p. 266].

The shadow, thus, is not wholly evil or bad. Good and evil are as close, for Jung, as identical twins. It is a moral problem that challenges the whole ego-personality. Moral effort is required in order to become conscious of it. It involves recognising the dark, sometimes criminal aspects of one's own being. As Jung states: "The shadow is a moral problem that challenges the whole ego personality, for no one can become conscious of the shadow without considerable moral effort. To become conscious of it involves recognising the dark aspects of the personality as present and real" (ibid. para. 14). The shadow has an obsessive, possessive quality (ibid. para. 15). Its dark characteristics have an emotional nature. On the lower level, one is uncontrolled, a passive victim to affect. In such cases of possession by the shadow, one behaves like a "primitive", "singularly incapable of moral judgement" (ibid.). With effort and insight, the shadow can be gradually assimilated into the conscious personality except where there are obstinate resistances, which are usually bound up with the emotionally-toned projections one invariably locates in others. The effect of projection is to isolate the individual from the environment. And though a man may recognise the relative evil of his nature, Jung opines that "it is rare ... for him to gaze into the face of absolute evil" (ibid. para. 19). So many things are vested in the shadow, including criminality. Someone must be convinced that he casts a very long shadow before he is willing to withdraw his projections.

Only when a man has experienced the power of evil and suffered accordingly will he relinquish his Pharisaic attitude to others, maintains Jung (CW 10, para. 867). Man needs to confront his own blackest shadow and all it contains and come to terms with himself, which is always a risk. "Anyone who perceives his shadow and his light simultaneously sees himself from two sides and thus gets in the middle" (ibid. para. 872). There is no good that cannot produce evil and no evil that cannot produce good. To make the shadow conscious entails encountering it, confronting it and assimilating it to consciousness.

The moral complex (the Freudian superego) is the bedrock of character and culture. The shadow, on the other hand, comprises all those unacceptable and stigmatised, unactualised or repressed aspects of the Self, including criminality. Literature is replete with shadow characters—Faust, Jekyll and Hyde and Mephisto. Their badness allures, their evil attracts. These criminal characters from fiction as well as the real ones who walk our streets and enter our homes fall into and under the spell of the shadow and are possessed by it—in the grip of a shadow archetype, I think one could say. Such is my application of Jungian theory to criminality. Criminals, pale and otherwise, have failed to assimilate the shadow as any Jungian analyst would suggest. Faust, Mr Hyde and Mephisto act out those things we do not dare to do. As Stevens, the British Jungian observes, we prefer to behave like Dorian Gray (see Costello, 1996) putting on a persona for the world and hiding the evil in our nature. We entertain phantasies of forever losing the shadow and residing, without its spell, in some Marxian or Rousseauesque Utopia (see Stevens, 1982, p. 210).

The shadow, however, must be integrated within the total personality if its power is to diminish and finally fade. If those criminals could undergo Jungian analysis, they would gradually integrate components of the shadow. Stevens insists: "There is an urgent *biological* imperative to make the Shadow conscious" (ibid. p. 214). Jung provided the conceptual model which makes this "ontological triumph" possible (ibid.). It means acknowledging, accepting and owning those dark shadow aspects of oneself including the potential murderer that lurks within. It is to assume full personal responsibility for who one is. The darkness must see light but in the contained, sacred space of analysis. In as much as the Self includes unrealised positive potential, it has favourable therapeutic implications. After all, the Devil was, in fact, first a fallen angel (Lucifer).

Jung regarded the shadow complex as representing first and foremost the personal unconscious, but also as possessing an archetypal basis, the archetype of Evil, of Satan, but against this there is also the moral complex. The task incumbent upon us is to lessen the shadow's power through its conscious assimilation, which is precisely what the criminal has failed to do. The criminal exists in its spell, gripped, possessed, taken over. Jung insists on such an assimilation and working through of the shadow components, which include criminality.

> Such an experience brings about an inner transformation, and this is infinitely more important than political and social reforms which are all valueless in the hands of people who are not at one with themselves. This is a truth which we are forever forgetting, because our eyes are fascinated by the conditions around us and riveted on them instead of examining our own heart and conscience. Every demagogue exploits this human weakness when he points with the greatest possible outcry to all the things that are wrong in the outside world. But the principle and indeed the only thing that is wrong with the world is man [CW 10, para. 441].

In order to change and engage in ethical acts one must be *conscious*. Consciousness is a prerequisite for morality (see Costello, 1995). Integration of the shadow is the hallmark of ethics. In criminal cases, the criminal is identified with his shadow—Mr Hyde has taken over Dr Jekyll. Freedom from the shadow's spell occurs when one's criminality and aggression are not repressed in the shadow but admitted to consciousness and "worked through" in the process of analysis. The key lies in dealing with the shadow without becoming possessed by it. I am here reminded of the "Star Wars" trilogy in which an archetypal battle between good, as represented by the young handsome Jedi knight, Luke Skywalker and evil, as represented by the dark, masked Lord Darth Vader, is played out. Vader was a former Jedi knight, but the power of "the dark side of the force" exerted a terrible pull over him until finally he acceded to possession by the shadow. Man must consciously own the personal shadow and assume responsibility for the archetype of evil.

However, far too frequently, Wotan, the barbarian within, bursts out like Jung's teutonic blond beast ripping apart the social and ethical fabric of life and engaging in Hitlerian programmes of senseless savagery and chronic criminality. In our own days we have witnessed the genocide perpetrated in Bosnia and Rwanda, murderous paedophilia in Belgium, serial killing and cannibalism in America, mass murderers in Australia, fratricide in Argentina, bloody apartheid in South Africa, terrorism in Iraq and Northern Ireland, and the Frederick West and James Bolger cases in Britain.

Horror heaped on horror. The criminal subject's structure remains unpolarised between persona and shadow. In short, the criminal *is* his shadow. To conclude this chapter let me stress once again that the shadow must achieve consciousness if its spell is to be finally smashed. Such a task is surely Sisyphean.

CHAPTER THREE

Klein: the severity of the superego

"He sticks his fingers into the wound ... He plunges both hands into the meat ... he digs into all the holes ... He tears away the soft edges ... He pokes around ... He gets stuck ... His wrist is caught in the bones ... Crack! ... He tugs ... He struggles like in a trap ... Some kind of pouch bursts ... The juice pours out ... it gushes all over the place ... all full of brains and blood ... splashing ... He manages to get his hand out ... I get the sauce full in the face ... I can't see a thing ... I flail around ... The candle's out ... He's still yelling ... I've got to stop him! ... I can't see him ... I lose my head ... I lunge at him ... by dead reckoning ... I hit him square ... The stinker goes over ... he crashes against the wall ... smash! boom! ... I've got my momentum ... I'm coming after him ... I give him a good kick in the ribs ... I give him a good smack in the puss ... He collapses ... He quivers like a rabbit ... then he stops moving completely"

Louis-Ferdinand Céline, *Death on the Installment Plan*

M elanie Klein (1882–1960) was one of the most prominent psychoanalysts of this century. She changed the Freudian terrain with her conceptualisations, pioneering child analysis. If Freud found that the child was father to the man, Klein found that the infant gave birth to the child and the man. Before examining Klein's position on criminality in detail, it is necessary to adumbrate her unique contribution to contemporary psychoanalytic thought by elucidating a number of specifically Kleinian concepts in so far as she differs from and deepens Freud's work in several crucial respects.

Key Kleinian concepts

Klein stressed the emotional life of the infant during the first few years of life. She especially emphasises anxiety, unconscious phantasy, early object relations, which are crucial in determining subsequent development and the four central mechanisms of defence in particular: splitting, projection, introjection and projective identification. According to Klein, the first object is the mother's breast and the infant's relation to it is initially as to a part object. Both oral libidinal and oral destructive impulses are directed to the mother's breast. There is an interaction between love and hate corresponding to the (con)fusion between the life and death instincts which, according to Klein, are innate. Love is an expression of the life drive while hate, destruction and envy are emanations of the death drive. The introjected good breast becomes a vital part of the ego. As a representative of the life instinct within, it strengthens the infant's capacity to love his objects, reassuring against and assuaging anxiety. Likewise, the introjected bad breast represents the death drive and becomes a persecutory internal object linked to aggressive impulses and instincts.

Persecutory anxieties are characteristic of what Klein calls the *paranoid–schizoid position* (Klein, 1946), which is predominant in the first few months of life, (the first trimester of the first year). It consists not only of schizoid withdrawal but also destructive impulses, which, by projection, cause and create external persecutory objects and a splitting mechanism of the mother figure into a very idealised good part and a terrifying bad part.

Experiences of gratification and frustration are stimuli for love and hate. The breast (which is both the actual breast and a symbol of fulfilment and frustration), in so far as it is gratifying is felt to be good and in so far as it is frustrating is felt to be bad. The breast is split into two due to early lack of integration. Through introjection, a good and bad breast becomes established within the infant. The somatic experience forms the beginning of introjection; Klein stresses the somatic origins of phantasy. In projection, the infant expels and externalises his destructive impulses and attributes them to the frustrating, bad breast. He then experiences this object as wanting to hurt him. The first introjected objects, that is to say, the good and bad breast, form the core of the superego, according to Klein. In contradistinction to Freud, Klein holds that the superego starts with the earliest introjected processes. Idealisation and splitting are the primary defence mechanisms against persecutory anxiety at the paranoid–schizoid position. Objects become split as though they were two distinct objects, one ideal, the other persecutory. When persecutory anxiety is less strong, splitting is less severe. In schizoid types, progress toward synthesis is stunted. In depressive types, these divisions and dichotomies are less pronounced.

Greed and envy are the predominant phantasies in the paranoid–schizoid position. In its oral sadistic form, the desire is to deplete the mother's body of all that is good by introjecting it into the ego. In its anal form, the desire is to fill the mother's body with the bad parts of the self, which are split off and projected onto her, making her into a refuge and repository of what cannot be accepted or assimilated. But when I project my disowned and disavowed anger and aggression onto the external object, I experience the object as persecutory. In order to allay such persecutory anxiety I may have to re-introject my projections. I also project my good parts, either for safe keeping or for fear that my bad internal objects will damage and devour my good internal ones. In this way, the person is idealised and all that is good in me is denied. Both introjection and projection interact from the beginning of life; there is a constant dynamic interplay between these two intimately interconnected endopsychic processes.

With *introjective identification*, all the other's good parts are appropriated and incorporated in order to identify with them, thus creating a feeling of narcissistic omnipotence. On the other hand, in *projective identification* (mostly) anger, aggression, envy and hatred are projected and located it in an outside object (Klein, 1955, pp. 141–

175), which will then appear to persecute the subject, whose ego will feel depleted and diminished. The outside object now feels that there are alien parts/projections in him with which he may (unconsciously) identify. Identification by introjection and projection are, similarly, complementary and interactive processes. The concept of projective identification has been developed by authors such as Bion, Meltzer, Rosenfeld, Joseph and others. Bion, in particular, substantially developed the concept by distinguishing between normal and pathological projective identification (Bion, 1955a, pp. 220–239; 1955b, pp. 266–275; 1959, pp. 308–315).

Klein discovered a complex inner world consisting of innumerable objects incorporated into the ego, corresponding to good and bad figures. These figures, originally split at the paranoid–schizoid position, are slowly integrated by the ego in its development towards the depressive position. The *depressive position* (Klein, 1935 and 1940) is a period extending from four to six months, according to Klein, during which the infant's relation with others becomes more differentiated, more integrated. Splitting becomes less absolute as separate parts move together into a synthesis. The ideal mother becomes a mixed figure, no longer perfect but felt to be damaged by the former sadistic phantasies. Concern sets in (reparation). The infant both loves and hates the same object (ambivalence), which is loved in spite of its bad parts. Depressive rather than persecutory anxiety is the main emotion at this stage, which reinforces the desire to make reparation as the infant's ego attempts to inhibit the aggressive impulses and exhibit libidinal ones instead. The ego will continue to utilise defences from the paranoid–schizoid position, such as denial, splitting and idealisation, in an attempt to counteract the depressive anxiety. In other words, there is a regression. However, these defences become less extreme in the depressive position and may alter in form. There are now the manic defences against the depressive anxiety such as omnipotent denial of the importance of the loved object, which becomes denigrated (Klein, 1940). To summarise: the movement from the paranoid–schizoid position to the depressive position is the transition from part to whole-object relationships; from persecutory to depressive anxiety; from envy and greed to guilt, reparation and mourning; the attainment of which, according to Klein, is a life-long achievement. Furthermore, it is not as if all the former defences are finally overcome in an Hegelian synthesis. The dialectic is one of discontinuity, one of fluidity rather than fixture. In this respect, it is more Kierkegaardian than Hegelian. (One question we could ask is: Is he who has reached the depressive position less likely to become a criminal, possessing as he does, *depressive guilt*?).

I feel that the above, necessarily condensed and over-simplified, excursion and explication of certain crucial Kleinian concepts is justified and indeed essential in order to appreciate and understand Klein's conceptualisations on criminality, to which we will now turn our attention. Briefly stated, Klein viewed the violent crimes committed by adults as resembling the phantasy wishes of young children, which were externalised due to unconscious guilt. We will now explore this in much greater detail.

Normal Children(?): from the neurotic to the criminalistic

In her paper, "Criminal Tendencies in Normal Children" (1927, pp. 170–185), Klein shows how we can see criminal tendencies at work in every child and she suggests that these tendencies may assert themselves subsequently in the personality structure. Klein begins by stating that repression is directed against the most antisocial "murderous tendencies" (ibid. p. 170 and 1963, p. 279) of mankind. According to Klein, child analysis reveals how early on the fight takes place between the cultured and the primitive parts of the personality. From the earliest beginnings, introjection and projection are operative and are the basis for the internalisation of the mother's breast both in its good and bad aspects. It is this internalisation which is the foundation of the superego. Her researches conclude that the superego is operative as early as the second year. At this stage it has passed through both the oral sucking and the oral biting fixations—the latter being connected with cannibalistic tendencies. The fact that babies bite the mother's breast is evidence, according to Klein, of this fixation. In the first year there can also be glimpsed the anal–sadistic eroticism, where the infant gains pleasure from the anal erotogenic zone together with its concomitant pleasures of cruelty, mastery and possession. These oral and anal sadistic instincts and impulses, which have a constitutional basis (Klein, 1957, pp. 176–180), contribute to the criminal tendencies inherent in so-called normal children, according to Klein.

In contrast to Freud, Klein's Oedipus complex occurs at the end of the first and at the commencement of the second year. In her conceptualisations, it plays the largest part in the development of the personality, determining who will become a neurotic, a psychotic, a pervert or a delinquent. It also coincides with the depressive position. In the second quarter of the first year of life, the child enters into the positive and inverted Oedipus complex. Klein's revision of the archaic, classical theory of the Oedipus complex includes its earlier appearance, a re-envisioning of female sexuality, a re-interpretation of penis envy and a recognition of a feminine complex in boys. Due to its inevitable complexity and density and the necessary limitations imposed upon this work, we have decided to omit further discussion of Klein's unique understanding of the Oedipus complex (see Klein, 1928, pp. 186–198 and 1945, pp. 370–419).

Character-formation is derived from Oedipal development, ranging "from the slightly neurotic to the criminalistic" (Klein, 1927, p. 171). Klein states: "In this direction—the study of the criminal—only the first steps have been made, but they are steps which promise far-reaching developments" (ibid.). The male Oedipal child, who hates his father as rival for his mother's affections, will direct his hatred, his oral–sadistic and anal–sadistic fixations at his first objects of desire. "Phantasies of penetration into the bedroom and killing the father are not lacking in any boy's analysis, even in the case of a normal child" (ibid.). As an example, Klein mentions a case of a very normal boy of 4 years of age called Gerald who had been brought to analysis solely for prophylactic purposes.

Two case histories

Gerald suffered from acute anxiety. One of his anxiety-objects was an animal which only had the habits of a beast but which was, in reality, a man. This beast that made big noises in the bedroom next door was the boy's father. "The desire of Gerald to penetrate there, to blind the father, to castrate and to kill him caused a dread that he would be treated in the same way by the beast" (ibid., p. 172). Gerald had a little tiger, which acted as his protector, but also proved at times to be the aggressor. Gerald proposed to send it into the next room to carry out his murderous desires on his father.

> In this case too the father's penis was to be bitten off, cooked and eaten, which desire derived partly from the boy's oral fixations and partly as a means of fighting the enemy; for a child, having no other weapon, uses his teeth as a weapon [ibid.].

The primitive part of his personality was represented by the tiger, which represented Gerald himself. He also had anal phantasies of cutting his father and mother to pieces and dirtying them with faeces. A dinner-party he arranged based on these phantasies resulted in a meal in which he and his mother were eating his father. Klein contrasts the primitive violence of these phantasies with that part of his personality, which was warm and kind-hearted.

Klein proceeds to mention an analogous case of a little girl whose rivalry for her father and the wish to take her mother's place in his love, led also to various sadistic phantasies.

> Here the wish to destroy the beauty of the mother, to mutilate her face and her body, to appropriate the mother's body herself ... is connected with a strong feeling of guilt, which strengthens the fixation to the mother [ibid.].

According to Klein, this complicated psychical situation becomes even more complex because the child appeals to its homosexual tendencies in defending itself against those drives, which the superego condemns, and develops an "inverted" Oedipus complex. This shows itself by a strong fixation in the little boy to his father and in the little girl to her mother. Later, this relation cannot be maintained and they withdraw from both and, for Klein, this forms the basis of an antisocial personality, because the relation to one's parents determines all subsequent object-relations. There is an additional determining factor and that is the relation to siblings. Analysis shows that all children suffer great rages of jealousy and rivalry in relation to both younger and older brothers and sisters. According to Klein, a very small child has an unconscious knowledge of the fact that children grow in the mother's womb and direct all their hate and jealousy towards this unborn baby, so that "we find desires to mutilate the mother's womb and to deface the child in it by biting and cutting it" (ibid. p. 173). Such sadistic desires produce a strong sense of guilt in the child. Since the objects it hates are also those that it loves, the conflicts that become apparent and which are burdensome for the superego lead to repression where the sadistic impulses remain ever active in the unconscious mind. This leads Klein to assert that "all the sufferings of later life are for the most part repetitions of these early ones, and that every child in the first years of its life goes through an immeasurable degree of suffering" (ibid.).

Envy and gratitude

Klein distinguishes between envy, jealousy and greed in her article, "Envy and Gratitude" (1957, pp. 176–235). Envy is the angry feeling that another person possesses and enjoys something desirable. Envious impulses set out to spoil or destroy it. It implies the subject's relation to persons and goes back to the earliest and exclusive relation with the mother. Jealousy is based on envy, involving a relation between at least two people and is concerned with love that the subject feels is due to him, but that has been taken from him by his rival. In this sense, one could say that envy is essentially dyadic while jealousy has a triangular and Oedipal structure. Greed, in Klein's dialectic, is impetuous and insatiable, exceeding what the subject needs and what the object is able to give. Greed aims at scooping out and sucking dry or devouring the breast. Its aim is destructive introjection, whereas envy not only seeks to rob but to put bad excrements into the mother's breast in order to destroy or spoil her. This destructive aspect of projective identification is operative from the beginning of life. The difference, however, is that while greed is mainly bound up with introjection, envy revolves around projection. Klein gives the example of the French legal system (ibid. p. 182) where crimes of jealousy carry less severe sentences probably because murder of a rival implies love for the unfaithful person. She cites the example of jealousy in *Othello* who "loved not wisely but too well". In his jealousy, he destroys the object he loves. "But jealous souls will not be answer'd so; They are not ever jealous for the cause, But jealous for they are jealous; 'tis a monster begot upon itself, born on itself" and "Oh beware my lord of jealousy; It is the green-eyed monster which doth mock the meat it feeds on" (ibid.). For Klein, the first object to be envied is the feeding breast. As St. Augustine described it in his *Confessions*: "I have personally watched and studied a jealous baby. He could not yet speak and, pale with jealousy and bitterness, glared at his brother sharing his mother's milk" (1992, p. 9). Enjoyment and the gratitude to which it gives rise, according to Klein, help to mitigate envious and destructive impulses. For Klein, the feeling of gratitude, (even if it is motivated by feelings of guilt), is a derivative of the capacity for love, which is closely linked with trust in good objects and presupposes the ability to accept and assimilate the loved primal object. Furthermore, gratitude is bound up with generosity (Klein, 1957, p. 189). Envy, on the other hand, is felt to be one of the greatest of the seven deadly sins because "it spoils and harms the good object which is the source of life" (ibid.). In this respect Klein quotes from Chaucer's *The Parsons Tale*: "It is certain that envy is the worst sin that is; for all other sins are sins against one virtue, whereas envy is against all virtue and against all goodness" (ibid.). Klein opposes life to envy and finds support for this in St. Augustine and St. Paul, the latter having stated, in the *First Letter to the Corinthians*, "love envieth not" (ibid. p. 202). For Klein, one of the consequences of excessive envy is an early onset of guilt (ibid. p. 194). If this premature guilt is felt to be persecutory, the object that rouses the guilt is turned into a persecutor. A stronger ego can bear the burden of such guilt and develop defences, namely and mainly, the tendency to make reparation and restitution.

Similarly in her paper "Some Reflections on *The Oresteia*" (1963, pp. 275–299), Klein maintains that the transition between the paranoid–schizoid and depressive position is the stage when guilt is essentially experienced as persecution (ibid. p. 286). Orestes, in the three tragedies of the Agamemnon, the Cheophoroe and the Eumenides, which comprise Aeschylus' *Oresteia*, can overcome his persecutory anxiety and work through the depressive position because "he never gives up the urge to cleanse himself of his crime" (ibid.). The more persecuted and guilty a person feels the more aggressive he may become, which will make him more likely to project the punishment outwards. Klein mentions the repeated sequence of crime and punishment, the Hellenic concept of *hubris* (insolence or pride) and *dike* (justice)—Pride and its Fall, Sin and Chastisement (ibid. p. 294). Klein states: "We have to believe that similar processes are operative in the delinquent or criminal (ibid. p. 290). In short, the superego can drive someone to commit crime (ibid. p. 294).

Children: further evidence

In *The Psychoanalysis Of Children* (1932), Klein similarly writes that fear of the superego may compel certain persons "to destroy their object and will form the basis for the development of a criminal type of behaviour" (p. 143). According to Klein, because crime springs from such early anxiety and feelings of guilt, the only hope of reforming the criminal is to analyse the deepest levels of the criminal's mental life (ibid.). Should such feelings of guilt become too overpowering their effect will once more be experienced as anxiety by the ego. Klein remarks: "If this line of thought is correct, then it would not be a deficiency in the super-ego but a qualitative difference in it that gives rise to a lack of social feeling in certain individuals, including criminals and so-called "asocial" persons" (ibid. p. 154). She further states that such asocial behaviour can be cured while the individual is still young (ibid. p. 282), at a time in childhood when such illnesses in future years cannot be readily foretold.

> It is impossible to know with certainty whether it [the illness] will turn into a psychosis, criminal behaviour, malformation of character or severe inhibition [ibid.].

According to Klein, severe and significant deterioration in character is more likely to occur to persons who have not established their first object securely and who cannot, therefore, differentiate between good and bad. In analysis with such asocial or destructive child-patients, the analyst can slowly resolve repression by interpreting the play and behaviour of the child, whose toys represent various significant people in the child's life such as mother, father, brothers and sisters. Klein states that any possible error about the meaning of the material is impossible due to the variety of the performances and she attests to the liberating and resolving effects of the analytic interpretations. Frequently after such interpretations of sadistic impulses the child will attempt to atone for what he has done by mending the toy doll he has broken or by fixing the toy train etc. Such reparative gestures can also be seen in the drawings and buildings etc. of the child. Klein is at pains to point out the close connection between these phantasies and the sexuality of children and the structure of the adult. Such sadistic and sexual phantasies, which lurk within *every normal child* can be carried into action by criminals and Klein gives the example of Jack the Ripper to support her thesis (1957, p. 176).

Klein is intent, in this paper, on illustrating the analogy between the crimes of adults and the corresponding phantasies she uncovered in the analyses of some small children. She cites the case, which was a combination of perversion and crime, of a criminal called Harmann who, after becoming intimate with young men whom he used in order to gratify his homosexual tendencies,

> cut off their heads, either burnt or disposed of the parts of the body in some way or other, and even sold their clothes afterwards. Another very horrible case was that of the man who killed various people, using parts of the bodies for making sausages. The analogous phantasies in children, which I mentioned before, had in all details the same features as these crimes. The persons on whom they were committed were, for instance, the father and brother of a little boy between four and five, to whom he was bound by a very strong sexual fixation. After having expressed the desired mutual masturbation and other actions, he cut off the head of the little doll, selling the body to a pretended butcher, who was to sell it for food. For himself he kept the head, which he wanted to eat himself, finding it the most tempting portion. But he likewise appropriated the belongings of the victim [ibid. p. 177].

Peter, the little boy in this case, was an obsessional neurotic who was dominated by severe oral and anal sadistic fixations. His libido was directed towards the father while his hatred was directed towards mother. However, since he was also very frightened of his father he could only maintain an object-relationship with his younger brother, which was ambivalent. Klein mentions that his need for punishment was great. In play, he represented himself and his little brother by two tiny dolls who were awaiting punishment from their mother due to their naughtiness. The mother, when she arrives, finds them dirty, punishes them and goes away. The two boys repeat their actions and are punished again. Klein relates:

> At last, the dread of punishment becomes so strong that the two children determine to kill the mother, and he executes a little doll. They then cut and eat the body. But the father appears to help the mother, and is killed too in a very cruel manner and also cut up and eaten [ibid. p. 178].

The two children then appear to be very happy but anxiety soon sets in when the killed parents come back to life. When the anxiety started the boy had hidden the two dolls under the sofa. The parents find the two dolls, the father cuts *his* head off, the mother that of the brother and they too get cooked and cannibalised. Klein informs us that this little boy subsequently lost his anxiety and became a socially well-adapted adult.

The analysis revealed that the change had occurred in his character during the summer, when the child had shared the parents' bedroom and had witnessed sexual intercourse. Because he had perceived this as being aggressive, his sadistic impulses were strengthened and he regressed to the pregenital stage of personality structure. The birth of a brother 6 months later likewise contributed to the conflicts he was experiencing. But what was most important in his psychosexual development was the feeling of guilt engendered by his superego, which was no less sadistic than his own fixations. The struggle between his sadistic superego and his sadistic impulses was too much of a burden for him. Though the superego is formed upon layers of unconscious identifications at the resolution of the Oedipus complex, the parents are not the sole source of the superego. Thus, the superego is not synonymous with parental prohibitions and prescriptions. It is partly structured on the child's own sadistic phantasies. The superego does not always coincide with the picture presented by a child's real parents (Klein, 1933, p. 249). The child can create phantastic images of its parents far removed from reality and develop "parental imagos that are peculiar to itself; though in every case they will be of an unreal and terrifying character" (ibid. p. 251). For Klein, the formation of the superego begins when the child starts to introject its objects orally.

Since the first imagos are endowed with the attributes of the intense sadism characteristic of this early developmental stage and projected into objects of the outer world, the child will become dominated by the fear of being attacked by these objects and from the imagined cruelty emanating from its superego. This anxiety increases its own sadistic impulses and the child will attempt to destroy these hostile objects. Klein summarises:

> The vicious circle that it thus sets up, in which the child's anxiety impels it to destroy its object, results in an increase in its own anxiety, and this once again urges it on against its object, and constitutes a psychological mechanism which, in my view, is at the bottom of asocial and criminal tendencies in the individual. Thus, we must assume that it is the excessive severity and overpowering cruelty of the super-ego, not the weakness or want of it, as is usually supposed, which is responsible for the behaviour of asocial and criminal persons [ibid.].

A severe superego

In her paper "On Criminality" (1934), Klein repeats the crucial point that it is not the lack of a superego, "but the overpowering strictness of the super-ego which is responsible for the characteristic behaviour of asocial and criminal persons" (p. 258). It would seem that she is talking about pale criminals. If the fear of the superego, either for intrapsychic or external reasons, cannot be allayed then the individual may be compelled to damage or destroy people "and this compulsion may form the basis for the development either of a criminal type of behaviour or of a psychosis" (ibid. p. 260). So the same psychological roots may develop either into criminality or into paranoia. As Klein observes: "Phantasies of persecution are common to both conditions; it is because the criminal feels persecuted that he goes about destroying others" (ibid.).

Repression makes it impossible for the child to abreact and sublimate these hostile phantasies in play. The feeling of guilt becomes heightened; the child repeats his misdeeds *ad nauseum*, which expresses his wish to be punished. Klein summarises: "This desire for punishment, which is a determining factor when the child constantly repeats naughty acts, finds an analogy in the repeated misdeeds of the criminal" (1957, p. 179). In the example given above, Peter and his brother were naughty and were punished. They then killed their parents and were in turn killed by their parents, and the whole process was repeated again. This repetition-compulsion is influenced by the feeling of guilt which demands punishment. The differences between the normal and the neurotic child are determined by the intensity of the fixations present, the manner and time at which they become connected with life experiences, the development and degree of severity of the superego and the child's innate, constitutional capacity for bearing such burdens and conflicts. According to Klein, there is no child who does not experience such fears and feelings of guilt which, furthermore, act as indicators of much greater disturbances in later life.

Klein now explicitly cites Nietzsche's concept of the "pale criminal" and observes that Nietzsche knew much about the criminal driven by his sense of guilt. Klein states:

> Here we come to the most difficult part of my paper: the problem of what development these fixations have to undergo in order to make the criminal. This point is difficult to answer, for the reason that psycho-analysis has not yet occupied itself much with this particular problem. Unfortunately I have not a great deal of experience to which I can refer in this very interesting and important field of work [ibid. p. 181].

The little criminal

Klein quotes one case which comes close to the criminal type. A boy of 12-years of age, who was sent to a reformatory, was brought into analysis with Mrs. Klein. His delinquencies involved destructive behaviour, stealing and sexual assaults on young girls. All his object-relationships were destructive, including same-sex friend-ships. He seemed uninterested in most things and indifferent to rewards and punishments. After only a few weeks in analysis his character began to change favourably, during which time he never committed any acts of delinquency. However, Klein was forced to break the analysis after two months for personal reasons and the boy began to behave in a delinquent fashion again during the break, whereupon he was sent back to the reformatory and all Klein's attempts to get him back to analysis on her return failed. She says: "I do not doubt in the least that he has started on the path of a criminal career" (ibid. p. 182).

Klein provides a succinct survey of the causes of his development. The boy had grown up under very desolate and difficult circumstances. His older sister had forced both him and his younger brother into sexual acts at a very early age. The father had died during the war, the mother had fallen ill and so this older sister had dominated the family. On the death of his mother, he was taken into foster-care and went from bad to worse. Klein asserts that the main factor in his development seemed to be fear and hatred of his sister. He hated his sister, "who represented for him the principle of evil" (ibid.), but to whom he was bound by a dominating fixation based on hatred and anxiety. But there were deeper causes for his delinquency. Throughout his childhood he had shared his parents' bedroom and had received a very sadistic impression from their sexual intercourse, which strengthened his own sadism. His desire for sexual relations with both mother and father remained under the domination of his sadistic fixations and was connected with acute anxiety. The violence of his sister assumed the place of his parents in his unconscious. He expected castration and punishment, the latter corresponding to his own primitive and sadistic superego. As Klein relates:

> It was plain that he repeated on the little girls the attacks that he had suffered himself, only changing the situation in so far that now he was the aggressor. His breaking open of cupboards and taking out articles, as well as his other destructive tendencies, had the same unconscious causes and symbolic meaning as his sexual assaults. This boy, feeling overwhelmed and castrated, had to change the situation by proving to himself that he could be the *aggressor* himself. One important motive for these destructive tendencies was to prove to himself again and again that he *was still a man*, besides abreacting his hatred against his sister on other objects [ibid.].

Klein mentions that his apparent indifference to punishment and fear was utterly misleading. On the contrary, he was overwhelmed by fear and feelings of guilt. His very strong and early repression deprived him of the possibility of sublimating his sadistic fixations.

Klein gives the example of sport where much sadism and aggression can be worked through in a sublimated and socially permissible manner (ibid. p. 183). She notes:

> In the case of the little criminal it was very interesting to see, as the repression was weakened through analysis, what sublimation took place. The boy, who had no interest but a destructive one of breaking and spoiling things, showed an entirely new interest in the construction of lifts and every form of locksmith's work. It may be assumed that this would have proved a good way of sublimating his aggressive tendencies, and that thus analysis might have turned him into a good locksmith, instead of becoming a criminal as may now be expected [ibid.].

Klein mentions that Hans Sachs, in a contribution to the psychology of the perversions, found that the conscience of the pervert is not less strict than that of the neurotic but that it was simply working in a different way. Similarly, Klein says that she found that the criminal did not possess a less strict superego than the neurotic, but that it was working in a different direction. So it is not the lack of a superego but a different development of it, which is the main factor involved in the disposition to criminality, according to Klein. She notes:

> It is just anxiety and the feeling of guilt which drive the criminal to his delinquencies. In committing these he also partly tries to escape from his Oedipus situation. In the case of my little criminal the breaking open of cupboards and attacks on little girls were substituted for attacks on his mother [ibid. p. 184].

At all times, however, Klein is intent on supplying us with details of the analogy between criminal acts and childish phantasies. Klein maintains that the capacity for love can be brought out in every child and that in the case of

> my little criminal, he was apparently utterly devoid of any capacity for love, but analysis proved that this was not so. He had a good transference to me, good enough to make analysis possible ... Moreover, analysis showed that this dull boy had a deep and sincere love for his mother. The mother died in terrible circumstances from cancer ... As she lay dead, the family was leaving. He [the boy] could not be found for some time: he had locked himself up with his dead mother in the room [ibid. pp. 184–185].

It is not easy to know where tendencies in a child will ultimately lead. "But precisely because we do not know we must seek to know. Psycho-analysis gives us this means. And it does more; it can not only ascertain the future development of the child, but it can also change it, and direct it into better channels" (ibid. p. 185).

Klein agrees that though it is notoriously difficult to cure the adult criminal, and that perhaps there are grounds for pessimism in this regard, experience has shown her that one can approach and cure both criminal and psychotic children. "It seems, therefore, that the best remedy against delinquency would be to analyse children who show signs of abnormality in the one direction or the other" (1934, p. 261).

Klein thought that child-analysis should become part of every person's upbringing, then perhaps the hostility and sadism, which spring from suspicion and fear, could give way to more social and "trustful feelings towards [one's] fellow-men, and people may inhabit the world together in greater peace and good-will than they do now" (1933, p. 257).

We conclude this chapter with Klein's observation that the pale criminal appears incomprehensible to the rest of the world due to his lack of love, but according to Klein this is only apparent (1934, p. 260). In analysis one always encounters love where there is hatred and hostility.

> Love is not absent in the criminal, but it is hidden and buried in such a way that nothing but analysis can bring it to light; since the hated persecuting object was originally to the tiny baby the object of all its love and libido, the criminal is now in the position of hating and persecuting his own loved object; as this is an intolerable position all memory and consciousness of any love for any object must be suppressed. If there is nothing in the world but enemies, and this is how the criminal feels, his hate and destructiveness are, in his view, to a great extent justified—an attitude which relieves some of his unconscious feelings of guilt. Hate is often used as the most effective cover for love; but one must not forget that to the person who is under the continuous stress of persecution, the safety of his own ego is the first and only consideration [ibid.].

Following on from Melanie Klein's conceptualisations, I outline below, in point form, my interpretation of the Kleinian position on pale criminality.

1. The crimes criminals commit often resemble the violent phantasies of young children.
2. Pale criminality represents the externalisation of unconscious guilt.
3. Crimes are, therefore, intimately interconnected to the superego and hence to the Oedipus complex.
4. Pale criminals possess severe superegos and suffer from persecutory anxiety characteristic of the paranoid–schizoid position.
5. Pale criminals are envious and have not reached or worked through certain aspects of the depressive position; they have failed to introject or securely establish good internal objects.
6. Among adult criminals, perverse sexual acts often accompany criminal ones (i.e. perverse criminals).
7. Clinically, there is a close connection between criminality and perversion, and criminality and paranoia.
8. Some subjects are more predisposed to criminality than others due to innate constitutional factors.
9. There is a possibility that "asociality" can be cured by analysis while the subject is still young.
10. Criminal tendencies are present in every "normal" child and, by extension, every "normal" adult.

CHAPTER FOUR

Winnicott: delinquency and deprivation

"I strike out at her with the already wet butcher knife that I'm gripping in my right hand, clumsily, slashing her neck from behind, severing something, some veins. When I strike out a second time she's trying to escape, heading for the door, blood shoots even into the living room, across the apartment, splattering against the tempered glass and the laminated oak panels in the kitchen. She tries to run forward but I've cut her jugular and it's spraying everywhere, blinding both of us momentarily, and I'm leaping at her in a final attempt to finish her off. She turns to face me, her features twisted in anguish, and her legs give out after I punch her in the stomach and she hits the floor and I slide in next to her. After I've stabbed her five or six times—the blood's spurting out in jets; I'm leaning over to inhale its perfume—her muscles stiffen, become rigid, and she goes into her death throes; her throat becomes flooded with dark-red blood and she thrashes around as if tied up, but she isn't and I have to hold her down. Her mouth fills with blood that cascades over the side of her cheeks, over her chin. Her body, shaking spasmodically, resembles what I imagine an epileptic goes through in a fit and I hold down her head,

71

rubbing my dick, stiff, covered with blood, across her choking face, until she's motionless"

Bret Easton Ellis, *American Psycho*

Together with Melanie Klein, Donald W. Winnicott (1896–1971), paediatrician, psychiatrist and psychoanalyst, was one of the giants of child analysis. He is representative of a characteristically British "object relations" school within psychoanalysis. Peculiarly Winnicottian concepts such as the "transitional object" and the "good enough mother" have entered the mainstream of the British school of psychoanalysis and influenced the Anna Freudians, the Kleinians and the Independents alike. It is his writings, though, on pale criminality which concern us here. Apart from one article entitled "Delinquency as a Sign of Hope" which was published in *Home Is Where We Start From: Essays by a Psychoanalyst* (1987), most of his major contributions to criminality have been collected in a volume entitled *Deprivation and Delinquency* (1984). As the title suggests, Winnicott's central idea in this work is that emotional (rather than social) deprivation can foster the "antisocial tendency", as he calls it, of delinquency. A delinquent is here understood as a young criminal—under the age of eighteen. We will draw extensively on this work.

Experiences with evacuation in wartime Britain

"Delinquency" is a term used to designate young criminals. We can, therefore, regard delinquency as synonymous with criminality. Much of the material for this work by Winnicott was written under the pressure of his experience in wartime Britain, where he witnessed many forms of deprivation and delinquency, particularly in his work with evacuated children (see especially part one of *Deprivation and Delinquency*, pp. 9–77).

Winnicott saw the character disorders as the clinical manifestations of the antisocial tendency of delinquency, ranging from bed-wetting and greediness to perversions and psychopathy. He traced the origins of delinquency, or at least the antisocial tendency, to specific deprivations in the infancy and early childhood of the individual. Prior to Winnicott, as we have seen, psychoanalytic theory had attributed delinquency and (adult) crime to guilt arising from unconscious Oedipal ambivalence. The central idea was that when guilt grew and accumulated and then failed to find an outlet in sublimation or reparation, something had to be acted out for the individual to feel guilty about. The aetiology of delinquency was seen in terms of the struggle within the inner world (psyche) of the subject. The focus was on intrapsychic rather than interpersonal configurations.

Applying psychoanalytic theory to the cases coming before him in his paediatric clinic, Winnicott, too, held that many childish symptoms and character disorders had their origin in these unconscious conflicts. However, though he emphasised the inner world of the child, he also saw environmental factors as decisive. His experience of the Second World War brought home to him the link between deprivation and delinquency. A subtle shift occurred, blending psychoanalytic theory with practical observation and experience.

For Winnicott, when loss (deprivation) is suffered, a manifest indication of distress and acting out (delinquency) is to be expected. Where no such reaction occurs, the disturbance is of a deeper kind. So Winnicott actually attached a positive psychological value to antisocial behaviour in children as a response to deprivation and loss. One important external factor in the causation of persistent delinquency, according to Winnicott, is a child's prolonged separation from its mother. Studies carried out of individual case histories confirmed the statistical inference that separation was the outstanding aetiological factor in cases ranging from mild behaviour disorders and physical illnesses to chronic delinquency. In particular, Winnicott stressed the fundamental importance of the family unit in the emotional development of the child's character. Often, when the home environment has failed the child, he will act out and engage in antisocial behaviour as a cry for help.

Winnicott had immense experience of working with children in hostels during wartime and in peace. He was employed by a county council from 1939 to 1946 in connection with a group of five hostels for children who were difficult to billet, where Winnicott had detailed knowledge of 285 children. Out of the evacuation experience, the general public became aware of the fact of antisocial tendencies and behaviour as a psychological phenomenon. Anti-social behaviour is a return of the repressed and a reminder of impulsiveness and of society's denial of the unconscious. Examples of the symptoms which occurred in the evacuation breakdown cases were: bed-wetting, faecal incontinence, stealing in gangs, burning of hay, train wrecking, truancy, signs of anxiety, maniacal outbursts, sullen and sulky moods, depressive phases, deterioration of personality with lack of interest in clothes and cleanliness and "insane" behaviour.

The residential management of such children constituted a therapy in itself and was supported by a psychiatric team who sometimes provided personal psychotherapy. Many of these difficult delinquent children had no satisfactory home of their own or had experienced the break-up of home or of a home in danger of breaking-up. All attempts were made to provide a suitable primary home substitute, where the child could have the experiences of loving and hating the same person, and of finding both his sense of guilt and his desire to repair and restore. Without this familial, physical, human environment the child cannot discover the extent to which his aggressive ideas fail to destroy, or come to know the difference between phantasy and fact. Without a father or mother together, he cannot express his desire to separate them. So, again and again, Winnicott empha-sises the crucial importance of a favourable familial environment in the healthy emotional development of the child in the first years of life.

Good hostel work, in which Winnicott was involved, attempted to protect the public from "nuisance" children, resolve public feelings of irritation, prevent delinquency and discover the best form of management and treatment for delinquent children in wartime emergency. The so-called "offences" of children were treated as signals of distress rather than indicators for punishment. In a proportion of cases, delinquency was definitely prevented and the child saved from ending up in Juvenile Court. The difficulties were dealt with as a matter of individual and social health and not merely as a matter of (unconscious) public revenge. Delinquency was treated as an illness and as a matter for psychological analysis and help, rather than punishment and penal institutionalisation.

The roots of aggression

As destructiveness is so often a part of delinquent behaviour it seems appropriate to begin a more theoretical account of the aetiology of delinquency by discussing Winnicott's account of the roots of aggression. In his two articles "Aggression" (1939) and "Roots of Aggression" (1964) in *Deprivation and Delinquency* (1984), Winnicott sees aggression as something inborn, co-existing with love. His ideas, in this respect, owe much to Melanie Klein who, in developing the ideas of Freud, pointed out, as we have seen, that it is the destructive urge in the child's inner world that turns into the desire to repair and assume personal responsibility. Departing somewhat from Klein, Winnicott maintains that aggressiveness at the very beginning of life is equated with bodily movement and with the establishment of what is and is not the self. Winnicott emphasises the importance of play and the use of symbols as a way of containing inner aggression and destructiveness. Winnicott believes it to be characteristic of the antisocial child that he has no area in his personality for playing. Rather, his capacity for playing is replaced by acting out.

From the start, love and hate co-exist and both involve aggression. Furthermore, sometimes aggression is a symptom of fear. In "Aggression, Guilt and Reparation" (1960), in the same volume, Winnicott links destructiveness with anger and frustration as well as hate and fear. A sense of guilt derives from toleration of one's destructive impulses (ibid. p. 142). Whatever is good and evil in the world of human relationships is, according to Winnicott, also found in the heart of the individual subject. In other words, in the infant there is both love and hate of full intensity. It is difficult to trace the origins of aggression. Sometimes, parents and teachers regard it as pent-up instinctual energy. To be sure, the infant possesses a vast capacity for destruction both in phantasy and fact. For Winnicott, the word "greed" conveys the idea of original fusion of love and aggression. According to Winnicott, firstly there is a primary greed or appetite-love, which may be cruel and dangerous, but it is only so accidentally. The infant's aim here is gratification. Secondly, there is a separation of what may hurt from what is less likely to hurt. For example, biting can be enjoyed separately from loving people through the biting of "objects" which cannot feel (pain or pleasure). The child must eventually learn to bring his personal inner and outer realities into harmonious integration. When the aggressive forces threaten to dominate the libidinal ones, the individual has to do something to save himself. What he does, according to Winnicott, is to turn himself inside out, to act the destructive role himself and bring about control by external authority. Otherwise, control within (the alternative) would result in clinical depression. The individual can then enjoy inner instinctual urges including aggressive ones, which form the basis for play and work. For Winnicott, aggressiveness nearly always represents the dramatisation of inner reality, which is experienced as too bad to tolerate. (Anna Freud in an unpublished paper makes the point that there is a relation between the giving up of masturbation and the onset of antisocial behaviour).

Sublimation, games (boxing and football, for example) and work obviously mitigate these intolerably destructive phantasies. Another manner and method for coping with aggressive instincts in the inner reality is the masochistic strategy whereby the individual suffers, expresses aggression, gets punished and so becomes relieved of guilt feelings and in the process experiences sexual excitement as well as gratification. If such adolescent aggression is not denied but integrated and accepted, it is then available to give strength to the work of reparation and restitution. As Winnicott relates: "At the back of all play, work and art, is unconscious remorse about harm done in unconscious phantasy, and an unconscious desire to start putting things right" (ibid. p. 91). It is, therefore, important to acknowledge, accept and even enjoy one's own cruelty, greed and aggression. Only then can such urges be harnessed to sublimated activity. To summarise: aggression has two meanings. In one way or another, directly or indirectly, it is a reaction to frustration (or deprivation). It is also one of the two main sources of an individual's energy. Because all individuals are essentially alike, as Winnicott maintains (ibid. p. 93), these features of love and hate in human nature can be located in all infants, as well as all children, adolescents and, indeed, in all people, independent of age, sex, race, skin-colour, creed or social setting.

Destructiveness appears commonly in a child's dreaming and playing as well as in his outward aggression, according to Winnicott. He observes:

We can see that these early infantile hittings lead to a discovery of the world that is not the infant's self, and to the beginnings of a relationship to external objects. What will quite soon be aggressive behaviour is therefore at the start a simple impulse that leads to a movement and to the beginnings of an exploration. Aggression is always linked in this way with the establishment of a clear distinction between what is the self and what is not the self [ibid. p. 94].

Of course, the vast majority of infants receive "good enough" care so that a certain degree of integration is achieved and the break-through of massive aggression and criminal destructiveness is staved and happily rendered unlikely.

The capacity for concern

In a paper dating from 1963 entitled "The Development of the Capacity for Concern" and published in *Deprivation and Delinquency* (1984), Winnicott sets out his fullest statement about the capacity in every individual to develop a sense of concern, and to assume personal responsibility for the aggressiveness and destructiveness that resides in man's own nature. Essentially, this is an adaptation of Klein's "depressive position". One difference is in the greater emphasis Winnicott places on the importance of the human environment, especially the mother, in meeting and nourishing the innate tendency and predisposition of the child towards concern and care. Winnicott believed that at the time when the capacity for concern is developing, from 6 months to 2 years of age, that deprivation can have devastating consequences. The beginning of the process of socialisation can be lost or "damned up" (see ibid. pp. 100–105).

Winnicott uses the word "concern" in a positive way in order to distinguish it from "guilt". He explains the differences thus:

A sense of guilt is anxiety linked with the concept of ambivalence, and implies a degree of integration in the individual ego that allows for the retention of good object-imago along with the idea of a destruction of it. Concern implies further integration, and further growth, and relates in a positive way to the individual's sense of responsibility, especially in respect of relationships into which the instinctual drives have entered [ibid. p. 100].

Concern refers to the fact that an individual cares and accepts responsibility. Concern emerges, according to Winnicott, at a period before the onset of the classical Oedipus complex, which involves a relationship between three persons. Winnicott describes the capacity for concern in terms of the mother–infant relationship. It constitutes a development belonging to a two-body relationship, a development depending on a "good enough" environment and "good enough mothering". The capacity to be concerned is a matter of health and presupposes a complex ego-organisation; it is an achievement. When the child has succeeded in combining its impulses, urges and experiences, erotic and aggressive and relating them to one object which is no longer split into two, then ambivalence (i.e. the depressive position) can be said to have been reached. The infant here is beginning to relate to outside objects and perceive the difference between subjective and objective realities, between "me" and "not me" elements. He has established a self, a unit that is physically contained in the body skin and psychologically integrated. There is an inside and outside to the child. The mother has become a "whole object" and the infant lives a psychosomatic life. The transition here is from splitting and the employment of crude defences, to reparation and the capacity for concern. The fact that everyone is capable of developing a sense of concern is hopeful but, as Winnicott has shown, so much depends on the earliest maturational processes and development of the child.

In his paper, "The Absence of a Sense of Guilt" (1966), again published in *Deprivation and Delinquency*, Winnicott links the idea of this damning-up of the capacity for concern directly with the antisocial tendency, and reminds us that social morality is a compromise. Here also Winnicott gives his view that the earliest morality lies in not betraying the "real" (as opposed to the "false") self.

Just as Freud alerted us to the concept of the superego formed by introjected parental figures, Klein developed the concept of early superego formations in the infant's mind which are relatively independent of the introjections of parents, as we have already discussed in chapter three. According to Winnicott, this is the origin of the sense of guilt. What, though, about the absence of the sense of guilt?

Winnicott draws our attention to the child affected by the

antisocial tendency who is in the process of becoming a delinquent. We are told, says Winnicott, that this boy (or girl) has no morality, no sense of guilt. Winnicott refutes this, however. In his psychiatric investigations of such delinquent children, Winnicott found a certain pattern (see ibid. pp. 110–111): (1) things went well enough for the child; (2) something disturbed this; (3) the child was taxed beyond capacity; (4) the child reorganised himself on the basis of a new though inferior pattern of ego-defence; (5) the child begins to become hopeful again and engage in antisocial acts in the hope of compelling society to return with him to the position where things went wrong and to acknowledge that fact; (6) if this is carried out, the child can return to the period before the moment of deprivation and rediscover the good object and the good controlling environment.

Winnicott completely abandons the notion that children are born innately amoral. This view entirely conflicts with Winnicott's observations of the maturational process and the facilitating environment. He proceeds to give an example of some schizoid patients who are, in some ways, more moral than we are. What is crucial in such cases is that they remain true to themselves. Winnicott observes: "Extra-marital intercourse is of no consequence to them as compared with betrayal of the self" (ibid. p. 111). For schizoid persons, wicked or wrong means anything that is false. Winnicott's distinction between a "true" and "false" self is reminiscent of Jung's concept of *self* and *persona*. Morality thus involves remaining true to one's true self. In relation to morality and guilt, Winnicott notes: "In the end you see I come down to the concept of a sense of guilt that is so fundamental to human nature that babies die of it, or if they cannot die they organise a compliant or false self which betrays the true self in so far as it seems to succeed in terms of what the onlookers believe to have value" (ibid. p. 112). He concludes this paper by reminding us that adolescent children are more concerned with not betraying themselves, that is to say, with remaining true to themselves, than with whether they smoke or sleep around etc.

(On a related theme: in "The Psychology of Separation" (1958), drawing on Freud's paper "Mourning and Melancholia" and on the work of Karl Abraham, Winnicott examines separation anxiety and the psychology of mourning and he demonstrates how mourning depends on the capacity to tolerate hatred of a person who has been loved and lost. Reaction to loss includes grief, mourning and depression, but when the loss occurs very early on in the child's life (prematurely), he or she cannot react properly to the loss. An immature ego is unable to mourn—mourning indicates maturity).

Crime as a psychological illness

In "Some Psychological Aspects of Juvenile Delinquency" (1946), reprinted in *Deprivation and Delinquency* (1984), Winnicott emphasises the destructive trend in delinquency—the seeking of a secure framework within which spontaneity and impulsiveness are safe. Here too Winnicott offers a description which links delinquency with deprivation of home life; this is seen to be the root of the delinquent's problem.

So often crime produces public revenge feelings. However, Winnicott is anxious to see psychological methods utilised in the investigation of court cases and in the management and treatment of antisocial children. Winnicott calls for a humane treatment of juvenile offenders. In short, he understands crime to be "a psychological illness" (ibid. p. 114).

What delinquents have in common is a deprivation in their home life. The early stages of emotional development are replete with potential disruption and conflict. The child's relation to external reality is not firmly rooted, the personality is not fully integrated and the infant's primitive love possesses a destructive aspect and aim. The child has not learned to tolerate his instincts. If the home fails to give a feeling of security to the child, he will look outside the four walls of his home so that instead of looking to his own family or school to provide support and stability, the antisocial child looks further afield to society. Winnicott writes: "I put it this way. When a child steals sugar he is looking for the good mother, his own, from whom he has a right to take what sweetness is there" (ibid. p. 116). He is also seeking to find the parental authority that can limit his impulsive behaviour and his acting-out. Winnicott's declaration that the child's acute need is for a strict father would seem to be in full agreement with the Lacanian position. The strict father may be loving but he also needs to be "strict and strong" (ibid.). "Only when the strict and strong father figure is in evidence can the child regain his primitive love impulses, his sense of guilt and his wish to mend. Unless he gets into trouble, the delinquent can only become progressively more and more depressed and depersonalised and eventually unable to feel the reality of things at all except the reality of violence. Delinquency indicates that some hope remains" (ibid.).

It is not necessarily an illness when the child behaves antisocially; antisocial or delinquent behaviour is at times "an S.O.S. for control by strong, loving, efficient people" (ibid.). Most delinquents are ill, Winnicott maintains. The delinquent offends against society (unknowingly) in order to re-establish control from outside. Most of these Winnicottian reflections are in accord with Lacan's observations. In contradistinction to the delinquent, the "normal" child develops a capacity to control himself (from inside) whereas the asocial child needs control from without, as he has not experienced a good "internal environment". Delinquency, Winnicott stresses, is an "illness of the individual" (ibid. p. 117). Failures come before the courts; successes become citizens. Winnicott asserts that in those criminal cases reaching the Juvenile Court to be tried for acts of delinquency, the Court could decide that what is needed is the provision of a strong and stable environment with care and love, accompanied by personal psychotherapy. But without the former, the latter is unlikely to succeed. Like Klein, Winnicott calls for properly trained psychotherapists to become available in such cases in order to supply much needed treatment especially in the more urgent and serious cases of criminality. Needless to say, children deprived of home life must be provided with something personal and stable and loving while they are still young enough to appreciate and use it or we, as a society, must provide suitable stability in the shape of an approved school or, failing that and as a last resort, the four walls of a prison cell (see ibid. p. 119).

The deprived complex and hope

Winnicott's 1956 paper, "The Antisocial Tendency", in *Deprivation and Delinquency* (1984), is his most definitive statement on the subject of juvenile delinquency. He describes the two trends in antisocial behaviour—stealing and lying on the one hand and destructive acts on the other, and he traces their origins in the lives of infants and children. This paper also contains the notion of delinquency as a sign of hope, a theme which Winnicott was to repeat in his 1967 article "Delinquency as a Sign of Hope" published in *Home Is Where We Start From* (1987), in which Winnicott summarises his main contention thus: "the antisocial tendency is linked inherently with deprivation" (ibid. p. 91). Things go well enough for the child, and then they do not go well enough. Some change occurs which alters the life of the child once he is old enough to appreciate such things. "The antisocial tendency relates not to privation, but to a deprivation" (ibid. p. 92). In such cases, the child reacts by engaging in acts ranging from the normal prank to the antisocial act. A stable and secure environment is immensely important. When a deprivation occurs in terms of a break-up of the home or an estrangement between the parents, something serious occurs in the child's mental organisation. His aggressive ideas and impulses become unsafe. This can result in an outburst of aggression and in acts of delinquency. The hope is that under analysis or even therapy, the child or adolescent will be able to relive the suffering that succeeded the reaction to the deprivation in relation to the person who is acting as psychotherapist, and to return to a period or memory of the time prior to the deprivation. In doing so, they can recall or recollect by reliving and thus abreact the result of the deprivation.

In "The Antisocial Tendency" (1956), Winnicott asserts that analysts of all persuasions have failed in the psychoanalyses of delinquents because treatment must be adjunctive to specialised environmental care. He writes that the antisocial tendency *"is not a diagnosis. It does not compare directly with other diagnostic terms such as neurosis and psychosis. The antisocial tendency may be found in a normal individual or in one that is neurotic or psychotic"* (ibid. p. 122). It is found in all ages and is intrinsically related to deprivation. Winnicott focuses on the deprived *child*. He observes:

> A child becomes a *deprived child* when deprived of certain essential features of home life. Some degree of what might be called the 'deprived complex' becomes manifest. *Antisocial behaviour* will be manifest at home or in a wider sphere. On account of *the antisocial tendency* the child may eventually need to be *deemed maladjusted*, and to receive treatment in a *hostel for maladjusted children*, or may be

brought before the courts as *beyond control*. The child, now a *delinquent*, may then become *a probationer* under a court order, or may be sent to *an approved school*. If the home ceases to function in an important respect the child may be taken over by the Children's Committee (under the Children's Act, 1948) and be given *'care and protection'*. If possible a foster home will be found. Should these measures fail the young adult may be said to have become a *psychopath* and may be sent by the courts to a *Borstal* or to prison. There may be an established tendency to repeat the crimes for which we use the term *recidivism* [ibid. p. 123].

Winnicott makes three further points: (1) the antisocial tendency is characterised by an element in it which compels the environment to be important (the patient unconsciously compels someone to attend to management); (2) the antisocial tendency implies hope (lack of hope is the fundamental feature of the deprived child but in the period of hope the child manifests the antisocial tendency); (3) there is a direct relationship between the antisocial tendency and emotional deprivation, typically in the period of late infancy and the early toddler stage (the age of 1 and 2 years) (see ibid. pp. 123–124). This last period is the most important. When there is an antisocial tendency there has been a real deprivation not simply a privation, as Winnicott stresses again and again. There has been the loss of something good in the child's universe.

Moreover, according to Winnicott, there are two trends in the antisocial tendency, which we have already referred to: one is represented in stealing, the other in destructiveness. Winnicott explains:

> By *one* trend the child is looking for something, somewhere, and failing to find it seeks it elsewhere, when hopeful. By the *other* the child is seeking that amount of environmental stability which will stand the strain resulting from impulsive behaviour. This is a search for an environmental provision that has been lost [ibid. p. 125].

To summarise so far: object seeking and destruction are the two trends at the early roots of the antisocial tendency, according to Winnicott. At the centre of the tendency is stealing, and lying, which is associated with it. According to Winnicott, the child who steals an object is not looking for the stolen object *"but seeks the mother over whom he or she has rights"* (ibid. p. 125), derived from the fact that the mother was created by the child (from the child's point of view). The union or fusion of the two trends (stealing and destruction), the libidinal and aggressive compulsions, is in the child and represents *"a tendency towards self-cure"* (ibid. p. 126). (We recall Jung's view that neurosis is an attempt at a new adaptation).

According to Winnicott, the first sign of the antisocial tendency is greediness. If we explore greediness we find the deprived complex. In other words, if an infant is greedy there is some degree of deprivation. (Of course, the mother will obviously fail to maintain a high degree of adaptation to id needs so that, in some way or another, every infant is deprived). "The greediness forms part of the infant's compulsion to seek for a cure from the mother who caused the deprivation. This greediness is antisocial; it is the precursor of stealing, and it can be met and cured by the mother's therapeutic adaptation, so easily mistaken for spoiling" (ibid. p. 127).

One important point Winnicott reiterates again and again is that at the roots of the antisocial tendency is a good experience that has been lost, at a time when the child's ego is in the process of achieving fusion of libidinal and aggressive id compulsions, to use Winnicott's language. He notes:

> Surely, *it is an essential feature that the infant has reached a capacity to perceive that the cause of the disaster lies in an environmental failure*. Correct knowledge that the cause of the depression or disintegration is an external one, and not an internal one, is responsible for the personality distortion and for the urge to seek for a cure by new environmental provision [ibid. p. 129].

Incidentally and interestingly, the antisocial tendency relates to acting-out, masturbation, pathological superego, unconscious guilt, stages of libidinal development, repetition compulsion, regression to pre-concern, paranoid defence and sex linkage in respect to symptomatology, but Winnicott deliberately omits any detailed discussion of these themes. He concludes the paper by pointing out that the treatment of the antisocial tendency is not psychoanalysis but the environmental provision of child-care. It is the environment that must provide opportunity for ego relatedness because "the child has perceived that it was an environmental failure in ego support that originally led to the antisocial tendency" (ibid. p. 131).

Adolescence and antisocial behaviour

In "Struggling through the Doldrums" (1961) and "Youth will not Sleep" (1964), both of which are reprinted in *Deprivation and Delinquency* (1984), Winnicott discusses the association between adolescence and antisocial behaviour. The "cure" for adolescent antisocial behaviour, as well as adolescence generally, is held to be the passage of time (the "maturational process").

Winnicott begins by establishing certain facts: the adolescent, who mistrusts compromise, does not want to be understood. Essentially, the adolescent is an isolate. Adolescence is a time of personal discovery and the establishment of an identity. Maturation is the only real cure for adolescence. Winnicott stresses the vital importance of the environment and the family setting. For the majority of adolescents the environment is "good enough" and they achieve adult maturity.

According to Winnicott, adolescence has violent potential (see ibid. p. 151). Violence and sex are inherent in adolescence. Adult maturity involves the transition from violence to physical prowess in athletics or to intellectual attainment. All adolescents go through a "doldrums area" in which they feel futile. Adolescence is characterised by a mixture of defiance and dependence. Parents are faced with problems of management at this time. Not only does the adolescent need to defy but also to prod society repeatedly so that when society's antagonism is made manifest it can be met with antagonism. The need to defy corresponds with one aspect of the antisocial tendency as it appears in delinquency (see ibid. p. 153). Delinquency is one type of illness, as Winnicott calls it, associated with adolescence. Winnicott observes: "Here again, there is a close relationship between the normal difficulties of adolescence and the abnormality that may be called the antisocial tendency" (ibid. p. 154).

At the risk of repetition let us again have Winnicott's main insight: at the root of the antisocial tendency there is deprivation, which may have involved the mother being depressed or withdrawn at a crucial stage, or it may have involved the occurrence of a break-up in the family. Winnicott states:

> Behind the antisocial tendency there is always a history of some
> health and then an interruption, after which things were never the

same again. The antisocial child is searching in some way or another, violently or gently, to get the world to acknowledge its debt, trying to make the world reform the framework which got broken up. In the root of the antisocial tendency is deprivation [ibid. p. 154].

Furthermore, if there is even one antisocial adolescent in a group, this produces a serial reaction and the others will cohere. This is a serious complication, as there is always the tendency in such cases to group violence, such as the world witnessed during the Nazi regime. Winnicott maintains that being an adolescent is difficult for anybody to bear, and enduring adolescence does indeed require bravery.

The antisocial tendency is present potentially or actually in nearly every adolescent, but the positive aspect to this is that the adolescent is attempting to reactivate a firm holding which was lost at some stage of childhood dependence. Winnicott concludes the paper thus: "Infinite potential is youth's precious and fleeting possession" (ibid. p. 158).

The practical management of delinquents

We began this chapter by examining Winnicott's experiences working with evacuated children in wartime Britain (which comprised the first part of his book *Deprivation and Delinquency*, 1984), then proceeded to explicate his main theoretical points regarding the nature and origins of the antisocial tendency (part two of his book). We now conclude this chapter by considering the practical management of difficult children including the provision of psychotherapy (which covers parts three and four of his book).

Winnicott looks at the juvenile delinquent from the point of view of which type of social provision would be of most help in the individual cases and he discusses punishment versus treatment and therapy. A number of factors are addressed which we will simply enumerate, as most of them have been discussed in detail already. (1) Winnicott makes the point that it is doubtful whether the psychoanalytic treatment of delinquents or criminals will ever become valuable to the community (ibid. p. 164). (2) Quoting convincing figures from Bowlby, Winnicott shows how separation can augment the tendency to the development of a psychopathic personality. (3) The deprived child is ill, a person with a past history of traumatic experience (ibid. p. 177) ("I regard every offender as ill", ibid. p. 202). (4) In the provision of the deprived child, psychotherapy may be added but it is not practical politics. The essential procedure is the provision of an alternative to the family— foster parents, small homes in the care of preferably married wardens, humane hostels where the goal is truly therapeutic and detention centres. All these facilities are important in the group management of maladjusted children.

Appropriate "cover" needs to be found. Winnicott explains: "The antisocial child has two alternatives—to annihilate the true self or to shake society up till it provides cover. In the second alternative if cover is found then the true self can re-emerge, and it is better to exist in prison than to become annihilated in meaningless compliance" (ibid. p. 195). [In passing, one should point out that the "transitional objects" such as teddies, books or a bit of blanket the child carries around, enables him to withstand frustration and deprivation (ibid. pp. 186–187)].

According to Winnicott, treatment must go hand in hand with punishment. We cannot, nor should not, think only in terms of treating the criminal. The law cannot give up punishing all criminals (see ibid. pp. 202–203). That said, it is unlikely that punishment will be effective. Winnicott observes: "Society demands that the individual be punished. The individual being ill is not in a state to derive benefit from punishment, and is indeed most likely to have to develop pathological trends, masochistic and other, for dealing with the punishment as it comes" (ibid. p. 205).

However, residential care, if equipped with a good team, frequently acts as therapy, according to Winnicott. He proceeds to set out the differences in the therapeutic needs of the psychotic, the neurotic and the delinquent. He again links deprivation with delinquency and its two trends of lying and stealing. He also shows, through the spontaneous drawings of a child patient, the nature of a specific deprivation. Deprivation may dominate in "normal", neurotic or psychotic persons (ibid. p. 238). For example, the antisocial tendency (which may crystallise into delinquency) can be seen in a healthy, "normal" child who, at the age of two, takes a coin from his mother's purse. But as Aristotle noted, one act of thievery does not make a man [or in this case, a child] a thief. There are normal minor delinquencies in every home—all children damage household property, for example (see ibid. pp. 259 and 261).

The antisocial tendency, arising from a deprivation, "represents the child's claim to get back behind the deprivation to the state of affairs that obtained when all was well" (ibid. p. 242). It comes as "an S.O.S., *a cri de coeur*, a signal of distress" (ibid. p. 247). The aim in the treatment is to arrive at the original trauma to re-establish and renew a relationship with good objects that had been lost or broken. As Winnicott states: *"The patient needs to reach back through the transference trauma to the state of affairs that obtained before the original trauma"* (ibid. p. 248).

Dissociation, denial and partial disintegration is characteristic of the antisocial boy or girl. Guilt may be admitted but is not felt. One difference in the sexes is that adolescent girls tend to demonstrate their antisocial tendency by prostitution (ibid. p. 251). Winnicott summarises:

> In pathological antisocial behaviour the antisocial boy or girl is driven to mend, and to make the family or society mend, the failure that has been forgotten. Antisocial behaviour belongs to a moment of hope in a child who is otherwise without hope. At the point of origin of the antisocial tendency is a deprivation, and the antisocial act aims at a mending of the effect of the deprivation by a denial of it … In the antisocial tendency there was an initial period of satisfactory personal development; and then there was a failure of the facilitating environment, this failure being felt, even if not intellectually appraised, by the child [ibid. p. 260].

The treatment or therapy must be inaugurated before a hardening sets in, which is associated with delinquency in the public mind. Winnicott concludes by giving a fascinating account of a psychotherapeutic session with a girl of 8 years—Ada—who was brought to him on account of stealing (see ibid. pp. 262–282). Winnicott includes her drawings for our analysis. It shows the resolution of her compulsion to steal. The interview with Winnicott may not have produced a conscious insight or a confession, Winnicott admits, but it did produce a healing.

Winnicott's major contribution to our understanding of delinquency was in showing its intimate and intrinsic link with emotional deprivation at an early age. His diagnosis of deprivation: "The deprived child or relatively deprived child has had environmental provision that was good enough so that there was a continuity of personal being, and then became deprived of this: deprived at an age (in emotional development) at which the process could be felt and perceived" (ibid. p. 212). Such deprived and delinquent children are said to be maladjusted and in the grip of the "antisocial tendency".

CHAPTER FIVE

Lacan: the symbolic mistaken for the real

> "I called up executioners in order to bite their gun-butts as I died. I called up plagues, in order to suffocate myself with sand and blood. Bad luck was my god. I stretched myself out in the mud. I dried myself in the air of crime. And I played some fine tricks on madness"
>
> Arthur Rimbaud, *A Season in Hell*

J acques Lacan (1901–1981), a disciple of Freud's turned creator, initiated a radical re-reading of Freudian psychoanalysis in the light of the new science of structural linguistics. In his article in the *Écrits* (1966) entitled "Introduction théorique aux fonctions de la psychanalyse en criminologie" (1950) and recently translated as "A Theoretical Introduction to the Functions of Psychoanalysis in Criminology" (1996), Lacan sets out his psychoanalytic views on criminality. According to Lacan, the criminal acts in the Real order in a symbolic fashion. In order to understand what Lacan means by this, it will be necessary to elucidate Lacan's epistemological triad of the Real, the Symbolic and the Imaginary, as it pertains to his interpretations on pale criminality. In what follows I shall stay close to Lacan's own words.

The Real (R), the Symbolic (S) and the Imaginary (I) orders are tied together like three shoelaces—vital, necessary and intimately interlinked. Lacan likens these orders or registers to the Borromean knot. The Borromean knot is so called because the figure is found on the coat of arms of the Borromea family. It is a group of three rings, which are linked in such a way that if any one of them is severed all three become separated. All three threads are interconnected and interwoven. Further rings can be added without abdicating the Borromean quality. Lacan utilises the Borromean knot in order to illustrate the interdependence of the three orders.

Though the three orders are heterogeneous, referring to distinct areas and aspects of psychoanalytic experience, each order can only be defined in its relation to the other two. They are concerned with mental functioning and cover the entire field of psychoanalysis, the structural interdependence of which is captured by the Borromean knot. Let us explore the three orders in more detail beginning with the Symbolic and concluding with Lacan's description of the Real.

The symbolic order and the Oedipus complex

According to Lacan, the subject has a place in a kinship structure before he was born. From Lévi-Strauss and Mauss, Lacan was especially influenced by the idea that the social world is structured by certain laws which regulate kinship relations, and the exchange of gifts. As a subject, he is situated as an element in an unconscious, complicated network of symbols. Symbols and words envelop the subject and help to constitute him in an unconscious structure. In "The Function and Field of Speech and Language in Psychoanalysis" (from 1953) and published in the Écrits: A Selection (1977a), Lacan observes:

> Symbols in fact envelop the life of man in a network so total that they join together, before he comes into the world, those who are going to engender him "by flesh and blood", so total that they bring to his birth, ... the shape of his destiny, so total that they give him the words that will make him faithful or renegade [Lacan, ibid. p. 68].

The Symbolic order is language, culture, ritual and myth. Communication is the basic form of exchange (the gift of the word).

The Symbolic is a linguistic domain but language involves imaginary and real aspects in addition to its symbolic dimension. The symbolic dimension of language is that of the signifier. The Symbolic is also the realm of radical alterity, of the Other, as Lacan terms it. It is that which is larger than the individual and into which we have to accommodate ourselves; compromise is called for. It is also the realm of the Law, which regulates desire in the Oedipus complex; it is the realm of culture rather than nature. It is characterised by triadic structures because all intersubjective relations are mediated by the big Other. The Symbolic order is also the realm of death and lack. In *The Seminar. Book ii. The Ego in Freud's Theory and in the Technique of Psychoanalysis, 1954–1955* (1988), Lacan speaks of the Symbolic order as a universe.

> In the symbolic order the totality is called a universe. The symbolic order from the first takes on its universal character. It isn't constituted bit by bit. As soon as the symbolic arrives, there is a universe of symbols [ibid. p. 29].

It is impossible to speculate on what preceded the Symbolic order other than by symbols. Only by working at the level of the Symbolic can analysts effect or evoke changes in the analysand. The psychoanalyst is, thus, compelled to penetrate beyond the Imaginary and work within the confines of the Symbolic.

The human subject is blind to his destiny. He can live like another, unaware of his history, or he can discover the truth for himself, the truth for and of the subject. This process of discovery consists in a gradual unravelling and unveiling of the discourse that founded him and the stripping bare of all the illusions that structured his path. The Symbolic order is social, public and intersubjective. What permits it to function and what keeps the subject anchored in it is the Name-of-the-Father, which is absolutely necessary in order to give structure to the symbolic. The No/Name-of-the-Father (*Non/Nom-du-Père*) refers to the prohibitive role of the non-biological, metaphorical "father" who is the bringer and bearer of the law and language and lays down the incest taboo in the Oedipus complex.

> It is in the *name of the father* that we must recognise the support of the symbolic function which, from the dawn of history, has identified his person with the figure of the law [Lacan, 1953, p. 67].

Lacan plays on the homophony of *le nom du père* and *le non du père* to emphasise the legislative and prohibitive function of the Symbolic father. The Name-of-the-Father, as a symbol of the law of incest prohibition, stands for the first social imperative of renunciation. The Name-of-the-Father is a fundamental signifier which confers identity on the subject in that it names and positions him within the Symbolic order and signifies the Oedipal prohibition.

As Freud defined it, the Oedipus complex comprises an unconscious set of sexual and hostile desires harboured by the subject in relation to his parents. According to the Freudian formulation, the subject desires one parent and enters into intense rivalry with the other. In the "positive" form, the desired object is the parent of the opposite sex and in the "inverted" form the desired object is the same-sex parent. For Freud, as for Lacan, the Oedipus complex emerges in the third year of life and declines in the fifth year, approximately. Like Freud, Lacan regards the Oedipus complex as the central one in the unconscious but he differs from Freud on a number of crucial points. For Lacan, the Oedipus complex is the paradigmatic triangular structure, the key function of which is the father. The Oedipus complex can be seen as the transition from the Imaginary to the Symbolic.

In this symbolic constellation, the mother's function differs from the father's. The mother (or her image) stands for the first object of the child's narcissistic anaclitic attachment and self-love, beginning a type of mirroring relationship, which Lacan labels the Imaginary. By contrast, the father utters a "no" and forbids the child to take repossession of that which he once possessed. This renunciation by the childish subject implies a repression of his desire, meaning that the child will substitute other objects of desire, to which he can only have access through the acquisition of language. When the child is learning how to speak, this incestuous desire is displaced onto substitute signifiers of desire. This is what the Oedipus complex accounts for mythically. It constitutes the Symbolic through the coincidence of the child's introduction to language and the constitution of his unconscious. When the subject begins to speak, he demands and every demand is, ultimately, a demand for love. All speech is demand. It is insatiable. This is why one does not appeal to the subject at the level of his demands but at the level of his desire. And desire is in the Real. The aim, it is said, of a Lacanian analysis is to lead the subject to the ecstatic limits of the "Thou art that", (ibid. p. 7) to the gates of moral choice.

Lacan discusses the concept of the "paternal metaphor" in relation to the Oedipus complex, which is his *point d'appui*. For Freud, all psychopathological structures can be traced back to a malfunction in the Oedipus complex, which is the nuclear complex of the neuroses. Lacan, likewise, relates the three clinical structures of the neurosis, psychosis and perversions (*père-version*) to difficulties in this complex. Needless to say, as a completely resolved Oedipus complex is impossible, so too is a completely nonpathological position. The closest would be a neurotic structure where the subject has passed through all three "times" of the Oedipus complex, which I shall discuss shortly. Psychosis, perversion and phobia result when "something is essentially incomplete in the Oedipus complex" (Lacan, 1954–1955, p. 201). In psychosis, there is a blockage before the first time of the Oedipus complex; in perversion the complex is carried to the third time but instead of identifying with the father, the subject identifies with the mother and/or the imaginary phallus. A phobia arises when the subject cannot negotiate the transition from the second to the third time of the complex because, as in the case of little Hans, the real father fails to intervene—the phobic object functions as a substitute signifier for the intervention of the real father.

The traditional view of the Oedipus complex concerns the literal genesis of the human subject's primordial and primitive desires such as incestuous sexual love for the mother and jealous murderous impulses manifested towards the father. Freud discovered a universal answer to the question: what does the human subject unconsciously desire? However, where Freud emphasises the "Oedipus" part of the equation, Lacan stresses the "complex". According to Lacan, there are structures, organised complexes and triangular systems. So the Oedipus complex is not viewed by Lacan solely in terms of sexual love, jealousy and rivalry, but also in terms of exchange and kinship structures. The family complex can be described as a socio–economic and symbolic structural positioning of the child in a complex constellation of alliance, in which the construction of desire, on the side of the mother and law, on the side of the father, is regulated through a linguistic structure of exchange, repetitive replacement and substitution of symbolic objects of desire.

Lacan places the function of the father at the heart of the Oedipus complex. The complex has a normative function in the moral structure of the subject, in his relationships and in the assumption of his sex. There are two terms operative here: virility and femination; a man assumes a virile type, a woman a feminine type. Lacan links the Oedipus complex to the function of the ego-ideal. In chapter nine, "The Paternal Metaphor I" of Book V of *The Formations of the Unconscious* (1957–1958), Lacan states: "There is no question of an Oedipus complex if there is no father" (ibid., p. 6) and "To speak about the Oedipus complex is to introduce as essential the function of the father" (ibid.).

In relation to the presence or absence of the father in the familial environment, Lacan makes the point that the father may be there (psychically) even when he is not there (physically). The father may possess a lack in the family and not in the complex. What is important for Lacan is the father's place in the complex. The father must intervene in the family and prohibit, not the child, but the mother. The Name-of-the-Father is linked to the primordial law of incest prohibition. Castration and the law are linked. Castration is linked to the symbolic articulation of the prohibition of incest and manifests itself on the imaginary plane. Because we harbour hatred and hostility towards the father whom we wish to castrate, we fear that he will do that to us. The fear before the father is centrifugal; it has its centre in the subject. The infantile subject imaginarily projects his aggressive intentions into the "father". The complex is a complicated dialectic of love and identification that remains ambiguous; its dissolution consisting in the subject identifying with the father.

In the "inverted" Oedipal position, the subject finds himself not with a healthy identification but in a passive position—he joins the ranks of the women, making himself loved by his father which involves the danger of castration, from which comes the form of unconscious homosexuality which possesses multiple consequences—a return of the homosexual position or its repression due to the castration complex. The castration threat is, of course, imaginary. Castration is a symbolic act whose agent is real. The father prohibits the mother from becoming the desired object of the child's desire. The mother is his, not the child's. Rivalry with the father engenders aggression in both male and female Oedipal subjects. The father frustrates the child with respect to the mother, the father *qua* symbolic father. He intervenes in so far as he makes himself preferred to the mother. This will lead, in time, to the formation, in the subject, of the ego-ideal.

The father is bearer of the phallus. The Oedipus complex culminates in privation. The female subject hankers (*penisneid* = penis envy) and the male subject should always be castrated if the Oedipus complex is to be resolved. The father who castrates is not a real object even though he has to intervene as a real object to embody castration. Neither is he an ideal object. The father is a metaphor. A metaphor is a signifier that comes in place of another signifier. And the function of the father in the Oedipus complex is to be a signifier substituted for the maternal signifier (S in place of S/). The mother may want the child, may have a desire for the child which keeps it alive, but she also wants something else, the x, the signified—the phallus. The child may make himself a phallus in order to become the desired object of maternal desire. There is always, though, a third party, the big Other. For Lacan, it is never a case of a dual relation. The child–mother–father triangle is fundamental. This symbolic triangle is instituted in the Real. The Oedipus complex can be seen, then, as the transition from the pre-Oedipal triangle of mother–child–phallus to the properly Oedipal triangle of mother–child–father. The Name-of-the-Father must be conferred on the childish subject. In the imaginary triangle, the child relates to the mother in so far as the child is dependent on the desire of the mother. The subject craves for her care, for contact and caresses, for her presence as well as for her desire. The subject is, thus, the desire of the desire of the mother. But she, too, desires something more, something other as she "pulsates" with life. This something more is the Symbolic order and the phallus around which the dialectic of object relations revolves. The phallus is a privileged object in the Symbolic order. The desire of the mother, as desire of the Other, involves this "beyond". In order to reach this beyond, this desire of the Other, a mediation is required which is given by the position of the father in the Symbolic order. The father in so far as he deprives the mother of the phallic object of her desire (which she does not possess), plays an essential role in the perversions as well as in the neuroses. The childish subject assumes or does not assume this privation, accepts or rejects the one who deprives the mother of the object of her desire. It is, thus, the nodal point of the Oedipus complex. The father "castrates" (symbolically separates) not the subject, as we have said, but the mother. The question is: to be or not to be the phallus. In order to have the phallus, it must first be possible not to have it. In that he accepts or does not accept it, the subject is led (man or woman) into being the phallus. At this stage, the father must intervene as promulgator of the law of incest prohibition. He speaks *ex cathedra* and the young subject is subjected to this law. We can summarise and paraphrase the three moments of the Oedipus complex thus, as outlined by Lacan in "The Paternal Metaphor I".

1. The first time of the Oedipus complex is characterised by the imaginary triangle of mother, child and phallus. Prior to the father's intervention there is never, for Lacan, just a dual relation between the mother and the child but always a third object present, the phallus as imaginary object of the mother's desire. In this first time, the subject realises that both he and his mother are marked by a lack. The mother is thus marred because she desires and the subject is likewise structured upon lack as he does not completely satisfy the mother's desire. What is lacking is the imaginary phallus. The mother desires the phallus, which she lacks and the young subject seeks to become the phallus for the mother, the object of her desire in order to fill her lack. Here what the young subject seeks is to be the desire of a desire, to be (or not to be) the object of his mother's desire. He introduces his demand. The child is the one from whom the demand emanates and the one in whom desire is formed. He will try to be this satisfying other/object for the m(O)ther. This is what Lacan calls the primitive phallic phase of perverse identification. In this first moment, the child relates not to the mother, as primordial big Other, but to the desire of the mother, to a desire of desire, to a mother's desire; this desire which is desired by the child. This desired object is the phallus seen as the metonymical object of desire, as a universal object for the subject, as a monument in place of a lack. The "I" of the mother becomes the child's other. The child identifies with the mother's object. The mother's desire is Law. But the real penile organ the child possesses is inadequate for satisfying such desire and it is

this incompleteness and impotence which gives rise to anxiety. Only the father's intervention in the later moments of the Oedipus complex can assuage such anxiety. So, the beyond of the mother must be established and become inscribed; this is constituted by her relationship with another discourse, that of the father, which the young subject must assume.

2. In the second moment of the Oedipus complex, the imaginary father intervenes as the one who deprives the mother by imposing law on her desire, by denying her access to the phallic object and forbidding the young subject access to his mother. The mother is, thus, symbolically castrated (the operation is one of privation). The demand of the Other is deferred, referred to a higher court. Here the law of the father is paramount. The mother is dependent on an object, which is not the object of her desire but an object that one has or does not have. She is in relationship with the Word of the father, in so far as what he says is not nothing. This second time is pivotal. It is when the father appears and makes himself felt as prohibitor in the mother's discourse. He may not be veiled but neither is he completely revealed. He prohibits, speaks a "no" to, proclaims a message of prohibition. At this second stage, the child's desire of the mother's desire is left in the lurch. The child becomes ousted in the second moment. He is no longer her metonymical object. He is expelled from paradise and complete possession. The childish subject now sees his father as a rival for the mother's desire.

3. In the third moment, the real father intervenes. The outcome of the Oedipus complex depends on this third moment. The father, as paternal subject and in so far as he is bearer of the law, must prove that he possesses the phallus. By demonstrating that he has the phallus, the (real) father "castrates" the child. He intervenes here as the one who has the phallus, not the one who is it and makes it impossible for the subject to persist in attempting to be the phallus for the mother. The father has the phallus and the young subject is freed from the anxiety of being the phallus for the mother. This reinstates the agency of the phallus as the object desired by the mother and permits the subject to identify with the father. The castration carried out is the privation of the mother, not the child. In the third moment,

the father can give the mother what she desires because he has it. It is the moment of the restitution of the relation of the mother to the father on the real plane. There thus occurs an identification with the father, as ego ideal, as he who has the phallus. The superego begins to be constituted here, formed out of this Oedipal paternal identification. At the moment when the father is internalised as ego ideal in the subject, the Oedipus complex begins to dissolve. The young subject does not, though, take up the exercise of his sexual powers immediately, but he has in his pockets, as Lacan puts it, the "title deeds". In so far as he is virile, a man is always his own metaphor. The father places himself, as locus of the law, above the signifying chain in a metaphorical position. For the male subject, it is a question of identifying himself with the father *qua* possessor of the penis and for the female subject it is a question of recognising the man *qua* the one who possesses it. The Oedipus complex can be seen, in short, as the conquest of the Symbolic order.

The imaginary order and the mirror stage

The Imaginary order is the register of illusion, deception, image, imagination, phantasy, fascination, seduction and lure. In mistrusting the imagination, Lacan comes close to a Cartesian rationalism. The Imaginary order relates to a dual relation between the ego and its spectacular image or *imago*. The basis of the Imaginary order is the formation of the ego in the "mirror stage", as theorised by Lacan in his 1949 article in the *Écrits*, "The Mirror Stage as Formative of the Function of the I as Revealed in Psychoanalytic Experience" (pp. 1–7). Identification is, thus, an essential element of the Imaginary order. For Lacan, the ego is an imaginary function, and is constituted as such at the "mirror stage" which takes place somewhere between six and 18 to 22 months in the psycho–sexual development of the subject. In the mirror stage, the ego is constituted by identification with the little other. The ego and the Imaginary order itself are, thus, two sides of a radical alienation. "Alienation is constitutive of the imaginary order" (Lacan, 1955–1956, p. 146). According to Lacan, the central structure of our experience belongs to the imaginary order, the data of which Lacan presented in 1936, drawing on Kohlberg, animal psychology and child psychology. The mirror stage is "a formative event in the life of a subject"; it is when a child is confronted with his reflection in a mirror and begins to recognise his image. The "mirror" may be a glass mirror or a mirroring person—the mother. The "mirror", in other words, serves as a metaphor. At this stage the infant (*in-fans* = without speech) is still in a state of motor uncoordination and incapacity, in a state of fragmentation. He feels himself, literally, to be "in bits". When he catches a sight of himself in a mirror, he will lean forward in "triumphant jubilation" so as to get into it. He perceives a whole and integrated image of himself, this image which can come and go with a slight change in the infant's position. So, pseudo-mastery is being set up, the mastery of that image will fill the infant with joy and triumph. Though he is still in pieces, by looking into the mirror he can anticipate a bodily wholeness and unity which, *in reality*, he has yet to achieve. In short, he identifies with this image in the mirror and falls in love with it (narcissism). The relationship between the ego and its counterpart is narcissistic. Furthermore, narcissism, which is another characteristic of the Imaginary, is always accompanied by aggressivity. In contrast to the auto-erotic stage in which a subject has a sexual relation to his own body, at this stage, the subject who has yet to speak takes the image of his *whole* body as a loved object. This *imaginary* idea of bodily integrity and mastery comes to him in the form of a *gestalt*, in "a mirage of the maturation of his power" (Lacan, 1949, p. 2). His movements and bodily immaturity are reversed in the mirror into, what Lacan calls, a "big statue of himself" (ibid.). In the mirror, everything is possible. It is, I think one could say, the place of all possible perversions. The subject, at this stage, moves from fragmentation and insufficiency to an illusory unity, from lack to imaginary wholeness. The illusions of the imaginary order are those of integration, autonomy, synthesis and similarity.

The mirror stage also situates the ego, the "I", before it is socially determined. It is constructed upon other and shifting identifications, on a line of fiction, which is difficult to undo or dismantle, except in analysis. It is the seat of first aggressivity. Why? The mirror stage sets up and erects total aggressivity à la Hegel's master/slave dialectic, as outlined in *The Phenomenology of Spirit* (1977). There is a fight to the death; the ego is locked in mortal combat with its double and one of them has to win. The spectacular image forces our aggressivity. (This has some parallels with Kleinian envy and projection. Once I project all my bad parts or even good parts into an other I begin, through projective identification, to feel persecuted by them and this, in turn, gives rise to the wish to destroy or spoil them). But we are not that image in the mirror. We, as speaking and sexual subjects, are not to be identified with our egos, Lacan asserts. The "I" is other, elsewhere, on another scene. We are not self-completed, enclosed or whole entities, "monads", to use Leibniz's expression; rather we are alienated self-divisions, according to Lacan. The subject is structurally split (*spaltung*). The mirror stage witnesses the beginnings of such an alienated identity. Lacan's message is that we will never be able to retrieve or return to the mirror stage. And the aim of a Lacanian analysis is to show up the deceits and falsehoods of the ego in the curse (*sic.*) of its development, to show that the ego, the "monumental construct of [our] ... narcissism" (Lacan, 1953, p. 40), at root, possesses a narcissistic and paranoiac structure whose "mastery" of the world is always illusory. That image carries us about and we become its slaves. The aim, or one of the aims, of a Lacanian analysis is to help us to break free from such a bondage so that we can discover a desire of our own and dare to desire.

The Imaginary order is, thus, the domain of mirror images, of (mirroring) relationships, reciprocities and identifications. In the mirror, any mirror, there is misrecognition, misconstrual, *méconnaissance*. That original identification which brought the ego into being is repeated through the Imaginary and reinforced by the subject in his relationship with external "reality". But my "I" is somewhere else. The "I" is both other, radically so, and another. The "I" is the subject of the unconscious, the subject of dreams, parapraxes, symptoms, bungled actions and unconscious desire. The ego has two faces or facets: the *ideal ego* of narcissistic sameness (here it will gather to itself more instances of sameness and resemblances in order to duplicate itself, beholden to the gaze of the other, to the lure of his look) (see Costello, 1996), and the *ego-ideal*, formed upon layers of other-identifications, especially the Name-of-the-Father, and which is located more within the structures of the Symbolic.

One consequence of this deeply clinical theorisation is that Lacan accused the other psychoanalytic schools of reducing analysis to the Imaginary order by making identification and even emulation with the being of the analyst the goal and end of analytic praxis. For Lacan, this is a complete deviation from and betrayal of Freudian psychoanalytic doctrine and technique. According to Lacan, the essence of analysis lies in its use of the Symbolic, which alone can disrupt and dislodge the disabling captivations and fixations of the Imaginary order. "The imaginary is decipherable only if it is rendered into symbols" (Lacan, 1956, p. 269).

The real order

The Real is a term used by Lacan in 1936 and revived in 1950 when he evokes Hegel's dictum "the real is the rational and the rational the real", (see Lacan, 1982, pp. 61–73). It becomes one of the three orders in 1953. The Real is *not* reality. Reality is a world organised through images and based upon the symbolic structures of language. It is easier to say that the Real *is*, than to say *what* it is. It is better understood by knowing what it is not. The Real is neither the Symbolic nor the Imaginary; it is opposed to the Imaginary and located beyond the Symbolic. It cannot be spoken of; it does not belong to language though language has some control and power over it. It is unassimilable to symbolisation. The Real is "that which resists symbolisation absolutely" (Lacan, 1953–1954, p. 66). The Real is "the impossible" (Lacan, 1977c, p. 167); it is impossible to imagine and to integrate into the Symbolic. There is an exclusion and voidance of all sense in the Real, an elision of meaning. The Real "is a moment of excruciating pain", as William Richardson, a Jesuit American Lacanian calls it. It is the locus of repetition and trauma. We only apprehend the Real gradually. It is essentially traumatic.

The Real belongs to the realm of death, desire and private *jouissance*. Like psychoanalysis, the Real is impossible; it is unimaginable, unstructured and defies expression of every kind. Where do we meet the Real? "For what we have in the discovery of psycho-analysis is an encounter, an essential encounter—an appointment to which we are always called with a real that eludes us" (Lacan, 1977c, p. 53). We have no words for it. It revolves around the trauma, encircling the hurt that shapes our lives. It may be the birth trauma, ("I'm alive, there's no cure for that", as Beckett exclaimed), or any shock we have had in the world and cannot symbolise. Phantasy is a way we try to deal with the Real. The neurotic subject has phantasies, which enable him to deal with the Real of trauma. The Real becomes repeated *ad infinitum* because it has not been symbolised. We can put this philosophically thus: he who has not examined his life is doomed to repeat it. (Socrates said that the unexamined life was not worth living).

We do not know why our lover left us, why the ladder fell on the child, why a loved one suffered then died. There is always a missed, avoided encounter. The Real is precisely this—when things break down, decompose, de(con)struct. In analysis, we deal with the patient/subject in his orientation to the Real in the first few face-to-face sessions as he attempts to rectify this Real. It is precisely this missed encounter with the Real that brings subjects into analysis and analysts are, or should be, according to Lacan, practitioners *par excellence* of the Symbolic.

Calderón once said: *"La vida es sueño"*—"Life is a dream". But life is not a dream and if we are living dreamily, Lacan tells us to wake up. The Real which is most real is other people, their mystery, their gestures, their strangeness and charm. In the Real of our world, we attempt to symbolise presence and absence, to present absence: the trail and the trace, footsteps in the snow, the burning bush. The madman and God keep each other company in the Real.

Acting out and passage à l'acte: some clinical considerations

After having explicated Lacan's epistemological triumvirate of the Real, the Symbolic and the Imaginary, let us now see how these concepts work within a criminal diagnostic. As we shall soon see, Lacan forged a new conception of the relation between criminology, psychiatry and penal justice, after the famous Papin sisters' case in 1933. This novel way of conceptualising criminal insanity would not find expression in Lacan's work in the 1930's, though it was already implicit in his doctoral thesis on Aimée and in his article on the Papin sisters published in a magazine called *Minotaure*. Lacan's compelling conceptualisations only came to doctrinal maturity in his address to the "Thirteenth Conference of French-language

Psychoanalysts on the Function of Psychoanalysis in Criminology",
20 years later in 1950. In this earlier work on homicide, Lacan
viewed violent crime as a self-punishing *passage à l'acte* associated
with a specific form of paranoia (see Lacan, "Aggressivity in
Psychoanalysis" [1948], *Écrits*, pp. 16 and 28). The paranoid
psychoses, manifested clinically by a delirium of persecution, are
accompanied by "characteristic criminal reactions" (Lacan, 'The
Problem of Style and the Psychiatric Conception of Paranoiac Forms
of Experience', *Critical Texts* 5.3, p. 5). Lacan further says: "Let us
also bear in mind that the criminal gesture of paranoiacs sometimes
stirs up tragic sympathy so much that the age, to defend itself, no
longer knows whether to strip such a gesture of its human value or
else to crush the guilty under its responsibility" (ibid. p. 6). *Passage à
l'acte* designates impulsive acts of a violent and criminal nature,
which occasionally marks the onset of an acute psychotic episode.
The passage to the act indicates the point at which the subject
proceeds from a violent intention or idea to the corresponding act.
Due to the fact that these acts are attributed to psychosis, French
law absolves the perpetrator of responsibility for them.

Lacan distinguishes between passage to the act and acting-out.
Both are last resort attempts at assuaging anxiety. However, the
subject who acts out still remains in the scene whereas a *passage à
l'acte* involves an exit from the scene altogether. Acting out is a
symbolic message directed to the Other, while a passage to the act is
a flight from the Other into the domain of the Real. The symbolic
network, the social bond, the signifying chain are dissolved in a
passage to the act. To highlight these important distinctions Lacan
draws on one of Freud's case histories, which we shall discuss
below.

A young homosexual woman

She was 18 years old, said to be both beautiful and clever and, with
devoted adoration and admiration, in hot pursuit of a "society
lady" who was 10 years older than herself. She had shown similar
feelings for a number of her own sex, and this had aroused her
father's suspicion and anger.

One day, as she was walking with this woman near her father's place of business, her father passed them by and cast them an angry look. This precipitated the girl rushing off and flinging herself over a wall on to a railway track. She fell down but survived this serious suicide attempt.

Freud discusses the details of this woman's case and the particularities of her female sexuality in his article: "The Psychogenesis of a Case of Homosexuality in a Woman" (Freud, 1920, pp. 145–172). The explanation she gave for her actions was as follows; because her father had prohibited the affair and the woman in question had failed to reciprocate her desire, she was in despair at having lost her loved one and wanted to kill herself. But according to Freud her attempted suicide was determined by two other motives, the fulfilment of a self-punishment and the fulfilment of a wish. The latter was the wish to have a child by her father; so it was her father's fault that she "fell". (There is a play in the text on the word *niederkommen*, which means both "to fall" and "to be delivered of a child"). From the point of view of *self-punishment*, the girl's actions show that she had developed strong unconscious death wishes against one or other of her parents, (against the father out of revenge for impeding her love and against her mother for becoming pregnant with her little brother). Freud treated her for a while but terminated the analysis, suggesting to her parents that she should continue to consult with a woman analyst.

This clinical case history is illustrative of a number of important analytical points. For our pedagogical purposes, I want to highlight one in particular that is evident in this case history—the difference between two clinical phenomena which are often confused, that is, *acting out* and *passage à l'acte* or passage to the act. By walking past her father's business premises accompanied by this society lady, the young homosexual woman was engaging in acting-out behaviour whereas the actual attempt at suicide constituted a *passage à l'acte*.

Lacan draws a distinction between *behaviour*, in which all animals engage, and *acts* which are symbolic and which he ascribes to human subjects. As actors we are to be held ethically responsible for our acts, both conscious intentional acts and the apparently accidental unconscious parapraxes. Psychoanalytic treatment differs from legal discourse in this respect: in law, a subject cannot be found guilty of murder, for example, unless it can be proved that the act was intended. In psychoanalysis, the analyst must assume responsibility in the treatment for his acts, interpretations and interventions, his words, sighs and silences. According to Lacan, an interpretation can be called a true psychoanalytic act when it expresses the analyst's desire. Neither acting out nor *passage à l'acte* are true acts since the subject does not assume responsibility for his *desire* in such actions. Lacan devotes his 1967–1968 Seminar entitled *The Psychoanalytic Act* precisely to these topics.

En passant, we may note that a bungled action is only partially successful because the desire is expressed in distorted and unconscious form. For Lacan, suicide is the only completely successful act since it expresses conscious and unconscious intentions, the conscious assumption of the unconscious death drive. However, a sudden and impulsive attempted suicide, as in the case we have just cited, is not a true act but a *passage à l'acte*.

Five years earlier, in his 1962–1963 seminar on *Anxiety*, Lacan discussed and differentiated between these two terms, acting-out and *passage à l'acte*, and so we will now turn our attention to this seminar.

In this seminar of January 1963, Lacan discusses this case history and argues that the father's irritated glance produced the *passage à l'acte*. But it is not enough to say this. Resentment and vengeance are present in the relationship between this young homosexual girl and her father. The scene that follows falls under the look of the father who embodies law and prohibits desire. There are many coordinates: supreme embarrassment, anxiety and, of course, the passage to the act, of which there are two conditions. Firstly, there is the girl's absolute identification with this *objet a* to which she is reduced. Lacan writes: "Confrontation with this desire of the father upon which all her behaviour is constructed, with this law which is presentified in the look of the father, it is through this that she feels herself identified and at the same moment, rejected, ejected off the stage" (ibid. p. 12). Secondly, there is the "letting (oneself) fall" or drop, which realises it. The letting drop is seen from the side of the subject. Later, Freud ends the analysis by letting her fall, by dropping her, through passing her on to a female colleague. This young homosexual passes, falls, into the Real. Such is a *passage à l'acte*. I hope that none of you who are reading this are dropping off!

Lacan continues his dense discussion. The passage to the act occurs at the moment of greatest embarrassment and with the behavioural addition of emotion in which the subject precipitates herself from the locus of the stage. She topples off the stage. This is the structure, as such, of the *passage à l'acte*, according to Lacan. This "escaping from the stage", this "exiting from the scene" distinguishes the *passage à l'acte* from acting-out. The woman in question jumps on to a semi-underground Viennese tramway. When Dora hears Herr K say to her: "My wife means nothing to me", she slaps him. They both pass into action. A fugue is another example of an exit from the scene. It places the subject in an infantile position. He throws himself into "this vagabond departure into the pure world, where the subject sets off to search for, to encounter something everywhere refused: he froths with rage" (ibid. p. 2). He returns, of course. Acting-out is different. As Lacan informs us: "In opposition to the *passage à l'acte*, all acting-out presents itself with certain characteristics which are going to allow us to isolate it" (ibid. p. 8). Commenting on both the case of the homosexual woman and Dora, Lacan distinguishes between the two terms thus:

> If the suicide attempt is a *passage à l'acte*, I would say that the whole adventure with the woman of doubtful reputation, who is raised to the function of supreme object, is an acting-out. If Dora's slap is a *passage à l'acte*, I would say that all the paradoxical behaviour, that Freud discovers immediately with such perspicacity, of Dora in the K's household is an acting-out. Acting-out, is essentially something in the behaviour of the subject that shows itself. The demonstrative accent, the orientation towards the Other, of every acting-out is something that ought to be highlighted [ibid.].

In our example, there is a show, something scandalous is staged before the eyes of everyone. It is public. It courts publicity. Because she can't have her father's child and she wants this child as a phallus, she fails in the realisation of her desire. She also makes herself a lover; she "establishes herself on what she does not have, the phallus, and to show clearly that she has it, she gives it. It is, in effect, a completely demonstrative act. She behaves, Freud tells us, *vis-à-vis* the Lady with a capital L, like a servant knight, like a man, as one who can sacrifice for her what he has, the phallus" (ibid. p. 9). There is a showing, a demonstrating and there is desire—desire to show oneself as other. Acting-out is, essentially, the demonstration, a veiled, though highly visible showing. Acting-out always demands the pound of flesh (the small *a*). Acting-out is a symptom; it shows itself as other and calls for an interpretation. Of course, acting-out cannot be interpreted directly; the transference is required. According to Lacan, acting-out is the beginning of transference (ibid. p. 11). Lacan describes it as "wild transference". There does not have to be analysis for there to be transference. "But transference without analysis is acting-out, acting-out in analysis is transference" (ibid.). A subject offers himself to his analyst's interpretation by acting-out. Acting-out is addressed to the Other and if one is an analyst, it is addressed to him. When a patient acts out an unconscious desire outside the consulting room, it can be seen as a resistance to the analysis but, from the Lacanian perspective, every resistance is first and foremost a resistance on behalf of the analyst himself. Lacan continues: "If he has taken up this place, so much the worse for him. He has all the same the responsibility which belongs to this place which he has agreed to occupy" (ibid. p. 13). Such is his desire and, perhaps, good fortune.

Acting-out occurs when the subject, in the grip of unconscious phantasies, relives them in the present with immediacy, usually out of synch with the subject's usual behavioural patterns. Freud's distinction between *repeating* and *remembering* is important in this regard. When past events are repressed from memory, they return in subsequent actions. When the subject does not remember the past, he is doomed to repeat it by acting-out. Acting-out concerns repetition. It results from a failure to recall the past. But it doesn't just consist of recalling something to consciousness, it also involves communicating this to an Other through speech. Acting-out occurs when recollection is rendered impossible through the refusal of the Other to listen. Because the Other chooses to be deaf or mute, the subject expresses the message in actions rather than words. So, acting-out is a ciphered message addressed to an Other who is unable to decipher it. The young homosexual woman was acting-out, by walking near her father's workplace, because what she was really doing was sending a message to her father who failed to listen to her. He had ears but he did not hear.

There are two further examples of *passage à l'acte* considered by Lacan. The first is the case of the murderous Papin sisters, which formed the basis for Genet's play, *The Maids* and was written

about by Lacan in the surrealist magazine *Minotaure*. The second is
the case of Aimée, a female psychotic patient of Lacan's, who
became a *cause célèbre* for the surrealists, and about whom he
wrote in his 1932 doctoral dissertation, "De la psychose para-
noiaque dans ses rapports avec la personalité" (1975) ("Paranoid
psychosis and its relation to the personality"), which we will now
briefly consider.

Aimée

Aimée was admitted to a mental hospital after attacking and
wounding a well-known Parisian actress with a knife. She did not
know the actress personally. When interrogated by the police, she
told them that the actress was spreading scandal about her and that
an associate, a famous writer, was revealing details about her
private life in a book. Aimée was suffering from delusions of being
persecuted, which cleared up after three weeks in prison, though
she spent a further 18 months in hospital, where Lacan obtained the
details of her history.

She was 38 years old on admission, separated from her husband
who had custody of their son. She had three younger brothers and
two older sisters and worked in the administration of a railway
company. Her father was tyrannical but Aimée had stood up to
him. She had a close relationship with her mother who seemed to
suffer from delusions of persecution as well. While her mother was
pregnant with Aimée, her eldest child fell into an open furnace and
died in front of her eyes.

She was seduced by the local "Don Juan" who later told her
that she was the object of a bet. She subsequently dreamed of being
with him for the next three years and became frigid in her
subsequent sexual encounters. She moved to Paris and the object
of her devotion became the object of her hate. For four years prior
to her marriage, Aimée had an intense and intimate relationship
with a female colleague from work who came, unlike Aimée, from
an aristocratic family but had fallen on hard times. It was from this
lady that Aimée learned the name of the actress she later stabbed,
for this actress was the neighbour of the friend's aunt and of Sarah
Bernhardt, whom the friend's mother knew. The two actresses

later became Aimée's major persecutors.

After a series of unsatisfactory affairs, she married a colleague but remained frigid and became pathologically jealous, staying mute for weeks on end. Eight months later, Aimée's eldest sister came to live with them after the death of her husband and began to dominate Aimée and take over her life. She filled a gap in Aimée's life and Aimée accepted her sister's domination. Throughout all this time, Aimée remained deeply ambivalent towards her sister, son, friends and husband.

Aimée's symptoms appeared when she was 28 years old when, after four years marriage, she became pregnant. She began to display extreme paranoia, believing that people on the street were whispering about her and criticising her conduct, and that newspaper articles were directed against her, threatening to murder her unborn child. She had nightmares of coffins. She also grew violent, slashing the tyres of a colleague's bike and throwing an iron at her husband. Her daughter was stillborn. This crystallised her hostile delusions even further.

The following year, she gave birth to a boy but during her pregnancy she was depressed and her delusions continued. She applied for a visa to go to the States, intent on making her fortune as a famous writer. She began to neglect her child and had delusions that her child had been taken away. Her family put her in a mental hospital where she remained for 6 months in an acute psychotic state experiencing delusions and now hallucinations. At her own request, she was transferred to Paris. The actress she later stabbed (not named in Lacan's thesis), Sarah Bernhardt, and a successful female writer became her main persecutors; she thought they wanted to harm her child. At this point, she herself began to write literary pieces for publication, in which can be seen her conflict. She hated famous people yet clearly wanted to be a famous writer herself. She wanted peace and brotherly love and longed for the reign of children and women who would be all dressed in white. She expressed her love for the then Prince of Wales in her two novels, poetry and letters, which she sent to Buckingham Palace.

She had a short period of "dissipation", as she called it, where she would stop men in the streets to tell them her ideas and to ask them whether they would sleep with her. A little later, she assaulted an employee of a publisher who had rejected her writings, for which she was fined. She returned to Paris, purchased a knife in order to defend her child from attack. She felt she had to *look* her enemy in the eye. She thought the actress would think of her as negligent if she did not show that she could defend her child. So she went to the theatre and assaulted the actress, and was then detained in prison, where her delusions persisted.

After 20 days she began to cry and her delusions disappeared. When she was admitted to hospital she spoke lucidly of her delusions and wrote Lacan a note. Lacan, for his part, relates the evolution of Aimée's delusions to certain events in her life and to the conflicts in her personality structure. Lacan hypothesised that her delusional system involved a deflection of hate from its direct object (her sister). This remained unrecognised by the subject as she continued to choose substitutes far removed from her sister, who was herself, of course, also a substitute for her beloved mother. Recognition (*reconnaissance*) took place at an unconscious level. The delusional system collapsed when Aimée moved from the delusional idea to the act, that is to say, when she wanted to look her enemy in the eye, which led to the attack on the actress, the *passage à l'acte*. By means of the stabbing, she turned her persecutor into a victim. What she stabbed was the symbol of her own idea. In this paranoid structure, the images were turned into internal persecutors and externalised as symbols. Interestingly, she felt relief after she was found guilty before the law and imprisoned, after which her delusions disappeared. This was because she was punished directly by the law and realised that the target of the attack was *herself*. Her paranoid structure had carried out an act of self-punishment, one could say. The wish behind the delusions was one of unconscious self-punishment in order to mitigate her enormous guilt over her attitude to her child. Lacan categorised it under a separate clinical category—"*self-punishing paranoia*", a term owing its origin to Freud's concept of "criminals from a sense of guilt". Lacan linked Aimée's conflicts to psychoanalytic concepts of psychical structure and personality development. He considered that there was a fixation at an early stage of super-ego formation. Lacan's thesis attempted (successfully) to make psychological sense of paranoid psychosis. He revealed that there is meaning in madness.

So we have examples of a young lesbian's suicide attempt, Dora's slap and Aimée's assault, all of which are clinical examples of *passage à l'acte*. Phenomenologically, there is a wide range of actions ordinarily classified as *passage à l'acte*, when the subject passes from an idea to the corresponding act, examples such as sexual assault and murder.

We are perhaps now in a better position to summarise and clarify the differences between acting-out and *passage à l'acte*. A *passage à l'acte* designates those impulsive acts of a violent or criminal nature, which occasionally mark the onset of an acute psychotic episode, as we saw in the case of Aimée. The phrase originated from French psychiatry and since the acts are attributed to the psychoses, French law absolves the perpetrator. We have all heard cases of the *crime passionelle*. Both acting-out and *passage à l'acte* are last resorts against unendurable anxiety. The difference is that in acting-out the subject is still in the scene, in the imaginary and symbolic theatre where phantasy is staged and played out. Acting-out is inscribed in the symbolic register. In contradistinction, *passage à l'acte* is a crossing over from the symbolic order into the Real where an alienation, more, an abolition of the subject ensues (in his identification with the *objet a*). So if acting-out is a symbolic message addressed to an Other, *passage à l'acte* represents a flight from the Other into the dimension of the Real. A *passage à l'acte* smashes the symbolic system, dissolving the social bond. It doesn't *necessarily* imply a latent psychosis but does involve a momentary dissolution of the subject (who becomes an object).

Later in his seminar on *Anxiety* (1962–1963), Lacan tells us: "The billygoat who jumps onto the stage, is what acting-out is" (p. 9). But there is also the stag and the fox, which we chase. Diana's hunt continues to this day. The Freudian thing is this Diana, which had to be continued by Lacan because what is missing in Freud's discourse is a question or, rather, an answer to a question: "What does Woman want?" This lack caused Freud to pass the young homosexual on, but the hunt goes on. As Lacan says: "The Freudian thing is what Freud let drop, but it is still what leads, in the shape of all of us, the whole hunt after his death" (ibid. p. 15). We continue the pursuit.

The criminal: his relationship to the real and the symbolic

According to Lacan, in his later article on criminality (1950), the object of criminology has two faces: (1) the truth of the *crime* in so far as the police are concerned; and (2) the truth of the *criminal* in his anthropological aspect. Lacan seems to be saying here that, as an analyst, he has something new to say about criminality, about that which has, up until now, been defined by psychology. Lacan is, thus, initiating a movement away from *conscious* considerations and conceptualisations towards unconscious ones. That said, Lacan agrees that neither crime nor criminals can be conceived of outside their sociological significance.

According to Lacan, there is a sociological reality to both crime and the law. He thus erects a dialectic between crime and the law. Drawing on St Paul, who stated that he would never have known what sin was but for the law, Lacan confirms that the law makes the sin, and that this is true outside the eschatological perspective of Grace in which St Paul formulated it. In the end, every society manifests its own relation of crime to the law by a series of chastisements and punishments, of which the realisation demands a "subjective assent" (ibid. p. 126), or acquiescence according to Lacan. In other words, punishment can only be carried out by an acquiescence on the part of the criminal. In effect, the criminal makes himself the executor of the punishment, which the law makes the price of crime. The penal code may demand different procedures but the subjective acquiescence is always required. The criminal, in other words, will be unconsciously saying: "I deserve this". This assertion comes under the term "responsibility". Punishment is thus ultimately derived from the notion of personal responsibility. Responsibility is an essential characteristic of the idea of the human.

The ethnologists have said that society is closed. Even primitively, if someone sinned, he would be held to have so little responsibility for his transgression that the law would exact satisfaction from his dependants. The criminal throws society into disequilibrium and so would be excluded or sent away, thus ridding society of the evil involved. According to Lacan, our present mores and customs carry traces of that collectivity in the sense that he who commits the crime is not held to be personally responsible.

Sometimes, society regards itself as so tainted in its structure that it excludes all such evil in the form of scapegoating. Furthermore, Lacan maintains that we have different images of the criminal, of what constitutes the criminal in his structure, depending on what court he is sent to. For example, we may imagine that the criminal sent to the Central Criminal Court would be more violent, more psychotic etc. than the criminal sent to the District Court.

Lacan here seems to be saying that in relation to sociological signification and conceptualisation, the analyst could collaborate unwittingly in the objectifying of crime due to these sociological references operating in society. In Lacan's view, civilisation and its discontents want to disjoin the coming together of culture (the external) and nature (the internal), while Lacan is seeking to conjoin them in the hope of making sociology less myopic.

Lacan is embracing an ethical position, which disavows deterministic excuses and states that we are all responsible for our actions. Recourse to the subject's confession is one of the keys to criminological truth and reintegration into the social community. Analytic (dialectical) dialogue confirms the absolute truth of the Pauline dictum: law makes the sin. Lacan draws on the dialectical dialogue of Plato's *Gorgias* where, within the rhetoric, there is present a concern for the just and the unjust. According to Lacan, Socrates exemplifies, in the truth of his being, his own maxim that it is better to suffer injustice than to do it. Socrates accepts his own destiny and submits himself to the enraged verdict of the court, which makes him a man. Freud spoke of the soft voice of the intellect which battles to be heard. Lacan speaks about the soft voice of the call of conscience which can still be heard by those who have ears to hear, in other words, for those like Socrates who are attuned to an ethics of being and behaving. Lacan comes down here on the side of Socrates as against society, on the side of justice as distinct from the law. Socrates cared for the inner word, which was the truth of his being. In Lacan's dialectic, there are two laws—one a positive law, and the other revealing itself as a "law of being", that is, as an ethics of desire.

One of Lacan's main points is that society contributes to the dehumanisation of the criminal. For Lacan, if psychoanalysis "de-realises" (the authors of the English translation render the term "de-essentializes") the crime, it does not dehumanise the criminal, and

crime expresses the symbolism of the superego as a psychopathological agency. Lacan believes that to explain a crime is neither to
forgive nor condemn it, neither to punish nor accept it. To explain a
crime is to *de-realise* it. In other words, it involves restoring it to its
symbolic dimension. For example, if the criminal is mad he is not
simply a monster, reduced solely to the level of his murderous
instincts and inclinations. If madness is to man what language is to
man, then there is no "nature" or "innate instinct", nothing "sub-
human" or "super-human" which is not already present in man.
We know that animals, acting out of innate instinctual behavioural
patterns, kill out of need or by nature, not out of sadism, which is
peculiarly human. (Of course, just because all criminals are human
does not mean that all crimes are identical. The structure of each
criminal differs in so far as he can be a neurotic criminal, a psychotic
criminal or a perverse one. Criminality, then, is not a discrete
nosological entity). Murderous rage, rape, torture, mutilation,
horror museums and concentration camps all belong to the realm
of mankind.

Prior to Freud, efforts were made to relate the criminal to his
physiological make-up. Lambroso's psychology was one such
effort. According to Lacan, Freud's depth-psychology was so
named because the psychology that preceded psychoanalysis was
so utterly superficial and simplistic. Lacan asserts that what was
novel in the Freudian revolution in relation to criminality was that
Freud discovered (unconscious) guilt. Lacan lambastes those people
who reduce psychology to its genetic formulation and objective
forms, which carry a behaviouristic experimentalism. Lacan also
goes further in maintaining that the madman is not lacking in
responsibility for his acts since madness is the alienated reality of
man, *à la* Hegel. So in abiding with Freud's original formulations,
Lacan de-realised the crime without dehumanising the criminal.
Thanks to Lacan, psychoanalysis resolved the enigma posed by
criminology by refusing the symmetry which pitted reason against
madness, man against beast and God against Satan. Lacan remained
true to the Freudian position, which was intent on separating
psychoanalysis from psychiatry. Lacan also refused the notion of so-
called "expert" psychiatric testimony, the aim of which was to
allow of no other alternative than to submit the criminal or the
madman to the categories of either reason or madness; and though

Lacan himself was a psychiatrist, he never gave "expert" testimony, thus refusing the discourse of the master.

In *Totem and Taboo* (1912–1913) Freud tried to show, in the first primordial crime, the origin of the universal law. According to Lacan, Freud recognised that mankind commenced with crime (incest and patricide to be precise) and with law. The modern figure of man is born in a Godless age, a moral man whose morality is derived from himself (the superego), from his own nature and not founded or dependent on religion. In this respect, even if it is true that "God is dead", as Nietzsche maintained in the *Gay Science*, this does not mean that "all is permitted", to quote Dostoevsky's maxim. According to Lacan, the call of conscience comes from within and so encompasses both the theist and atheist alike. And what the criminal is searching for, in his *ethical* way, is precisely punishment—self-punishment. His superego demands nothing less. For Lacan, the criminal's motives and the morbid structure of his crimes become obvious in the light of Oedipal interpretations because such is the origin of the superego.

Lacan states that "the structures of society are symbolic. Individuals, in so far as they are "normal", use them for *real* conduct ['behaviour' in the English translation]; in so far as they are psychopathic, express them by *symbolic* conduct" ['behaviour'] (1950, p. 132; 1996, p. 16). This is the key insight. Following Lacan, I think one could say that we "normal neurotic" subjects act in the Symbolic order in a real way whereas the criminal acts in the Real order in a symbolic way. We take the Symbolic as Symbolic; the criminal mistakes the Symbolic for the Real. He takes the structures of the Symbolic for something they are not. The psychopathological manifestations reveal the structure of a gap, a gaping hole, a rift in the Symbolic order. Psychoanalysis recognises delinquency as a psychopathology whose effects derive from the Oedipus complex. In the order of criminality, these psychopathological effects issuing from Oedipalism express a dehiscence in the family at the heart of society. The family, society and the conjugal couple are not functioning correctly. The father's function has broken down, collapsed. In such criminal cases, the triangular structure is ruptured and the father's function fails. Therein resides the tragedy.

Neurotic character is the reflection in the individual "of the isolation of the familial group of which these cases always demonstrate the asocial position" (Lacan, 1996, p. 17). The notion of "asociality" denotes the place of the criminal outside of the Symbolic. "It is thus that the criminal intentions included in the familial structure become pathogenic only in societies where the family situation disintegrates" (ibid. p. 18). This links up with Winnicott's insights.

Lacan then refers to Klein's researches, which affirmed the categories of "good" and "bad" at the preverbal stage of infantile behaviour. So it is a succession of crises which determine such dehiscence—weaning, intrusion (which Klein emphasises), Oedipus, puberty and adolescence. In relation to infancy, Lacan discovered the identification of the preverbal subject with the specular image at the mirror stage, a concept we have already explained. For Lacan, this is the original moment of the fundamentally alienating relation in which the human being constitutes himself. In relation to criminal behaviour, this stage's importance lies in the first signs of aggressivity that it erects, "I have also demonstrated that each of these identifications develops an aggressivity that cannot be adequately explained by drive frustration … Rather, this aggressivity expresses the discordance that it produced in the alienating realization" (Lacan, ibid. p. 21). So, aggressivity is set up at the mirror stage and can contribute to the potential criminal's antisociality and alienation. Lacan observes: "And this aggressive tension produces a type of object that becomes criminogenic in the suspension of the dialectic of the ego" (ibid. p. 21), Lacan showed the structural function of this object and its correlation with delirium in two forms of paranoiac homicide—the cases of Aimée and the Papin sisters.

In relation to the unconscious desire of the criminal to get caught and his compulsion to confess, Lacan notes that the criminal subject leaves behind a "calling-card", the flagrant "signature" left by the pale criminal. This fact is further strengthened by the recidivism of habitual criminals.

Lacan emphasises the social province, the social milieu or culture of the criminal. He stresses the symbolic co-ordinates. As he notes:

> The fundamental notion of an aggressivity correlative to every alienating identification allows us to recognize that there must be in

the phenomena of social assimilation, based on a certain quantita-
tive scale, a limit, where the standardized aggressive tensions must
be precipitated into points where the mass breaks apart and
becomes polarized [ibid. p. 23].

In other words, the *structural* aggressivity set up at the mirror
stage correlates with the *symbolic*/societal domain in which the
criminal is inserted as human subject. Criminality can stuff the
social body; the social body can produce the psychological type of
the criminal. Sometimes, in the very injustice of the city state
individuals can create themselves in their own image.

Commenting on the existence of so-called "criminal instincts",
Lacan cites the adage *homo homini lupus* (man is a wolf to man),
drawing, as he frequently does, on Balthazar Gracián, the Spanish
Jesuit writer of the Baroque era, who makes the point in his *Criticón*
that humans confronting one another exhibit far more ferocity and
aggression than carnivorous animals would ever be capable of. This
point is shared by the British Jungian Anthony Storr who writes in
the introduction to his book on *Human Aggression* (1968):

> The sombre fact is that we are the cruellest and most ruthless
> species that has ever walked the earth, and that, although we may
> recoil in horror when we read in newspapers or history books of the
> atrocities committed by man upon man, we know in our hearts that
> each one of us harbours within himself those same savage impulses
> which lead to murder, to torture and to war [p. 9].

And the British moral philosopher Mary Midgley similarly states in
her *Beast and Man* (1979) that ethological studies have established
that wolves are:

> by human standards, paragons of steadiness and good conduct.
> They pair for life, they are faithful and affectionate spouses and
> parents, they show great loyalty to their pack and great courage and
> persistence in the face of difficulties, they carefully respect one
> another's territories, keep their dens clean, and extremely seldom
> kill anything that they do not need for dinner. If they fight with
> another wolf, the encounter normally ends with submission. They
> have an inhibition about killing the suppliant and about attacking
> females and cubs. They have also, like all social animals, a fairly
> elaborate etiquette, including subtly varied ceremonies of greeting

and reassurance, by which friendship is strengthened, cooperation achieved, and the wheels of social life generally oiled [p. 26].

So it would seem that cruelty implies humanity. Love versus hate, the Hegelian fight to the death for pure prestige, which is peculiarly human.

Lacan concludes his paper on criminology by posing the question: "is not everything already weighed near the cradle in the incommensurable balances of Discord and of Love?" (ibid. p. 25). In this respect, perhaps we can be forgiven for thinking that, in the torrent of misdemeanours, thefts, pilferings, calumnies, rapes and crimes of murderous passion which confront society daily, Discord and strife are winning out over Love and harmony in the everlasting struggle, between this "battle of the giants".

CHAPTER SIX

Psychiatry: antisocial personality disorder

"What follows, down to the last detail, is my precise memory
of those events, for ever engraved on my mind through all
my suffering. I shall describe what happened—between two
zones of darkness ... Here is the scene of the murder just as I
experienced it. Suddenly I was up and in my dressing-gown
at the foot of the bed in my flat at the École normale ... it was
almost nine o'clock on Sunday the sixteenth ... Hélène, also
in a dressing-gown, lay before me on her back. Her pelvis
was resting on the edge of the bed, her legs dangled on the
carpet. Kneeling beside her, leaning across her body, I was
massaging her neck ... I pressed my thumbs into the hollow
at the top of her breastbone and then, still pressing, slowly
moved them both, one to the left, the other to the right, up
towards her ears where the flesh was hard. I continued
massaging her in a V-shape. The muscles in my forearms
began to feel very tired ... Hélène's face was calm and
motionless; her eyes were open and staring at the ceiling.
Suddenly, I was terror-struck. Her eyes stared interminably,
and I noticed the tip of her tongue was showing between her
teeth and lips, strange and still. I had seen dead bodies
before, of course, but never in my life looked into the face of

someone who had been strangled. Yet I knew she had been
strangled. But how? I stood up and screamed: 'I've strangled
Hélène!' "

Louis Althusser, *The Future Lasts A Long Time*

I n the concluding chapter, we will attempt a synthesis of the
diverse but related theories of pale criminality thus far
considered, but for a more complete picture of the aetiology
and phenomenology of pale criminality, we must first examine the
contribution of psychiatry, both orthodox and evolutionary.

In the *Diagnostic and Statistical Manual of Mental Disorders*, fourth
edition (the *D.S.M. IV*), published by the American Psychiatric
Association (1994), there is no entry under "criminality", for this
one must turn to the section on "antisocial personality disorder", a
generic term which covers criminality. Therefore, according to the
psychiatric medical model of mind, the criminal can be viewed as
suffering from "antisocial personality disorder". In what follows, I
will summarise the section from this influential psychiatric manual
before exploring the perspective of evolutionary psychiatry.

Personality traits are enduring patterns of perceiving, relating to
and thinking about oneself and the environment, and are exhibited
in a range of social and personal contexts. When these traits in the
personality become "maladaptive" or "inflexible" and cause
significant social or occupational distress and impairment, they
can then be said to constitute a *personality disorder*, which manifests
itself at adolescence, or earlier, and then continues throughout adult
life.

The essential features of "antisocial personality disorder" are: a
history of continuous and chronic antisocial behaviour in which the
rights of others are violated, persistence into adulthood of antisocial
behavioural patterns that began before the age of 15, and failure to
sustain job performance over a period of several years (obviously,
people like students or housewives would be unable to demonstrate
this particular feature).This pattern would also be referred to as
psychopathy (in Britain), *sociopathy* (in America) or "dyssocial
personality disorder". Individuals with "antisocial personality
disorder" fail to conform to social norms with respect to lawful
behaviour. They repeatedly perform acts which are grounds for

arrest. They are frequently deceitful and manipulative in order to gain personal profit or pleasure. They may repeatedly lie, use aliases, demonstrate patterns of impulsiveness; they tend to be irritable, irresponsible, aggressive and show little sign of remorse for the consequences of their actions. They do not make amends for their behaviour. They are lacking in empathy, tend to be callous, cynical and contemptuous of the feelings and sufferings of others. They tend to display inflated and arrogant self-appraisals; they may be excessively opinionated and self-assured and may display superficial charm, be verbally facile and exploitative in sexual relationships.

Typical early childhood signs of "antisocial personality disorder" may include the following: lying, stealing, fighting, truancy, sexual behaviour, excessive drinking and use of illicit drugs. After age 30 the more blatant aspects may diminish, such as sexual promiscuity, fighting, vagrancy and criminality. Associated features include signs of personal distress, such as inability to tolerate boredom and depression, the belief that others are hostile towards them and the inability to sustain lasting, loving, emotionally close and personally responsible relationships with family, friends and sexual partners.

In this "disorder", the subject may spend many years in an institution, more commonly penal than medical. Illiteracy and substance misuse are frequent complications. Predisposing factors include attention deficiency and unruly conduct during pre-puberty, extreme poverty and deprivation, removal from the home, and growing up without parental figures or the absence of parental discipline. These factors increase the likelihood that "character disorder" will develop into "antisocial personality disorder".

Age of onset is before the age of 15. It is more common in males than females. The prevalence for American men is put at 3% and for American women at 1%. It is more common in lower-class populations. Familial patterns and environmental influences are all important. "Antisocial behaviour" is attributed to those subjects engaged in criminal or similar behaviour who do not meet the full criteria for "antisocial personality disorder". In such cases, manic episodes may occur. Individuals with "antisocial personality disorder" also possess personality features that meet criteria for other "personality disorders" particularly "borderline", "histrionic" (hysterical) and "narcissistic".

As we will be discussing the hysterical structure from the point of view of evolutionary psychiatry, suffice it to briefly mention the so-called borderline and narcissistic "disorders". The latter is characterised by grandiosity, an insatiable hunger for admiration and phantasies of unlimited power, success, brilliance and beauty. Such people possess a strong sense of entitlement and need for approval; they are vulnerable to criticism and frustrated defeat, lack empathy for others and are frequently exploitative, demanding, arrogant and exhibitionistic. The so-called borderline suffers from emotional and affective instability, impulsiveness, hostility, self-injury, identity disturbance, recurrent suicidal ideation or behaviour, feelings of chronic emptiness, inappropriate anger, paranoid ideas, dissasociative symptomatology and show a frequent history of insecure parental attachments in childhood.

The diagnostic criteria for "antisocial personality disorder" as set out in the D.S.M. IV is as follows:

A. From the age of 15 years, there is a pervasive pattern of disregard for and violation of the rights of others, as indicated by three (or more) of the following:
   1. Failure to conform to social norms with respect to lawful behaviours as indicated by repeatedly performing acts that are grounds for arrest.
   2. Deceitfulness, as indicated by repeated lying, use of aliases or conning others for personal profit or pleasure.
   3. Impulsiveness or failure to plan ahead.
   4. Irritability and aggressiveness, as indicated by repeated physical fights or assaults.
   5. Reckless disregard for the safety of self and others.
   6. Consistent irresponsibility, as indicated by repeated failure to sustain consistent work behaviour or honour financial obligations.
   7. Lack of remorse, as indicated by being indifferent to or rationalising having hurt, mistreated or stolen from another.
B. The individual is at least 18 years of age.
C. There is evidence of the onset of conduct disorder before the age of 15.
D. The antisocial behaviour does not occur exclusively during the course of schizophrenia or a manic episode.

Evolutionary psychiatry

Turning now to evolutionary psychiatry. There have been innumerable paradigm shifts in the history of science. We have witnessed the Copernican revolution in astronomy, the Newtonian and Ensteinian paradigm shifts in physics, the Freudian and Jungian revolutions in psychology and the Darwinian paradigm of evolution in biology. A new conceptual framework for psychiatry has emerged in recent years based on Darwinian theory. This new emergent science, which combines the insights of ethology and sociobiology, defines human nature—its psychology and psychopathology—in terms of its evolutionary origins. It challenges the medical model of orthodox psychiatry which has been so pervasively influential but which has supplied few answers to the burning questions of mental health and illness. Evolutionary psychiatry is based on biological science. Jung's archetypal theory has been revisited, rediscovered and rehabilitated by some evolutionary psychiatrists who have introduced and adopted an ethological orientation to their work.

Historically, Niko Tinbergen's ideas of the 1950s (see N. Tinbergen, 1951) were expanded during the 1970s and the 1980s with the work of two sociobiologists, Charles Lumsden and Edward Wilson (see Lumsden and Wilson, 1983). Sociobiology, the term employed by Wilson, was based on the view that the survival of the gene determines the form of the behaviour studied. Many of the terms utilised by these thinkers, such as *epigenetic rules* and *pathways* and *innate releasing mechanisms* (I.R.M.s) are eminently compatible with Jung's archetypal hypothesis. The most important of the evolutionary psychologists and psychiatrists include Paul Gilbert, John Archer, Anthony Stevens and John Price of Britain and Russell Gardner, David Buss, Brant Wenegrat and Randolph Nesse of the United States. All have sought to place psychopathology on an evolutionary basis.

Should the "environment" fail to meet our archetypal imperatives and expectations, the "frustration of archetypal intent" ensues, to use Stevens's phrase (see Stevens, 1982), and this may result in psychopathology. Stevens and Price in their book, *Evolutionary Psychiatry* (1996), describe the process thus: "Psychopathology results ... when the environment fails, either partially or totally, to meet one (or more) basic archetypal need(s) in the developing individual" (p. 34). This view is in substantial agreement with attachment theory, developed by the British psychiatrist John Bowlby in the 1950s. Prior to Bowlby, it had been erroneously assumed and commonly accepted that attachment behaviour in infants was learned through conditioning and associated with the behavioural responses of rewards and punishments. The primary reward was food, which was thought to be responsible for evoking or eliciting attachment. This theory, known as the "cupboard love" theory, was accepted for decades by the vast majority of psychoanalysts, psychologists and psychiatrists, until Bowlby published his famous paper in 1958, "The Nature of the Child's Tie to His Mother". In this paper he attacked the cupboard love theory and suggested, instead, that infants might become attached to their mothers through *instinct*. Mother and infant, according to Bowlby, do not need to learn to love; they are innately and biologically programmed and predisposed to do so from birth. Let us take a closer look, then, at the family.

The family

The family has always been with us but it has evolved and changed down the centuries. The family is the fundamental unit in society. And the mother–child bond is crucial for healthy or "abnormal" psychological development. The infant's innate structures will anticipate, in some way, the behaviour of parents towards it. In *The Family Complexes in the Formation of the Individual* (1938), Lacan writes: "The family, at first approach, appears to be a natural group of individuals united by a twofold biological relationship: reproduction which provides the group with its constitutive elements and then certain environmental conditions necessary for the development of the young" (p. i). It is, thus, the primary *cell* of society.

As Lacan and others recognise, the human infant is born prematurely and is dependent on its mother for a substantial period of time. As the Jungian Erich Neumann puts it: "the mother's existence is the absolute life-giving and life-regulating precondition of infant existence, which alone makes its development possible" (1973, p. 17). After a period of time, the infant will be able to distinguish between "self" and "not-self" and comes to see the mother as a separate subject. In these early years, the formation of a secure attachment (or "base" in Bowlby's terms) to mother is crucial. It is only then that the child can form bonds with other significant objects—father, brother, sister, uncle, aunt, grandparents etc. The infant takes its place in the familial structure and begins to distinguish between friend and foe (the amity–enmity complex). The child will then explore his immediate environment and play and relate with his peers. Stevens (1982) sees the archetypal programme in terms of these three developmental stages: bond formation, stranger avoidance and exploratory activities (p. 86).

Optimally, there is a mother and a father and each exercises different functions. There is a hierarchical structure to the family, itself a complex structure, containing as it does, progeny, parenthood, laws of inheritance and succession, and laws of marriage; all of which are entangled with subtle and not so subtle psychological relationships. Lacan reflects: "the hierarchical structure of the family ... allow[s] us to recognise in it the privileged organ of the constraint which the adult exercises on the child, that constraint to which man owes a quite unique stage in his development and the primitive basis of his moral formation" (1938, p. ii). It is in the family that the child will first internalise external authority and which will form the basis, according to Freud, of its superego, which is formed upon layers of unconscious identifications beginning at the time of the resolution of the Oedipus complex. Culturally, the family is responsible for the moral education of its members. Lacan observes: "The family plays a primordial role among all human groupings in the transmission of culture ... the family is predominant in the first stages of education, in the repression of instincts and in the acquisition of that language which is quite properly called maternal" (ibid. p. iii).

A mother's libidinal investment (or cathexis, as it is called) in her child is evident from birth and before. It is only later that the father's function becomes apparent and is, indeed, crucial. The first object of desire is the mother's breast when the infant's ego is still in a rudimentary state. Lacan states:

> The weaning complex fixes the relationship of feeding in the psyche in the parasitic form that the needs of the infant human being

demand. It represents the primary form of the maternal imago [an imago is an unconscious representation]. From the beginning it is the basis of the most primitive and most stable sentiments which unite the individual to the family [ibid. p. 4].

Lacan writes of the "maternal embrace" and the "nostalgia for the nourishing breast on which the psychoanalytic school has been so equivocal", of a "fusional cannibalism" which "in the most highly developed love recalls the desire of the larva" (ibid. p. 8). So the early years are characterised by a positive biological deficiency due to the specific prematurity of human birth and overt dependency on mother. Lacan puts it thus:

> the image of the maternal womb dominates the whole of the life of a man ... In feeding, holding, and contemplating her child the mother, at the same time, receives and satisfies the most primitive of all desires. The tolerance of the pain of giving birth can be understood as a compensation which represents the first of the affective phenomena: the experience of anxiety which begins with life itself [ibid. p. 10].

So anxiety is the prototype of affect, which appears in the asphyxia of birth. And a little later, the infant's dependency can be seen "in the attachment of the child to his mother's apron strings and in the sometimes anachronistic duration of the relationship" (Lacan, ibid. p.11). This period immediately following birth is a sensitive one for successful bond formation to mother. For her part, the mother's attachment to her child strengthens and develops as the maternal agency seeks to fulfil the child's physiological needs to be fed, held and cuddled, in which can be heard the demand, insatiable as it is, for love.

The child soon establishes visual and auditory links with mother. He will single out the human voice, respond to the face of his mother at about the fourth week (he is equipped with the innate ability to smile and cry) and gradually attends to other environmental stimuli.

From the very beginning, the child's universe is dominated by the mother archetype, as Jung contended. This subtle and shifting repertoire of behavioural patterns and organisation, apparent in mother and child, represents the progression and gradual actualisation of the mother–child archetypal system, each stage of which is subjectively apprehended and comprehended. Erich Neumann has written extensively on the mother archetype in his book *The Great Mother: An Analysis of the Archetype* (1955). He maintains that certain expressions of this archetype are universally encountered: Mother Nature, Earth Mother, the Great Mother, the Devouring, Terrible Mother, Moon Goddess. The Great Mother is the central aspect of the archetypal feminine and like all archetypes possesses positive and negative attributes. The Great Mother is creative, caring, loving, nurturing as well as destructive, devouring and vengeful. Children are, thus, deeply ambivalent towards their mothers. The Great Mother and the Terrible Mother, in the classical Jungian schema, correspond to the "good" and "bad" breast, the good and bad introjected images of mother, as the Kleinians conceptualise it. Both aspects condition the child and the mother at an unconscious level. Neurosis, psychosis, perversion and, of course, delinquency and general personality disturbance are consequences of prolonged separation from mother and/or loss of significant attachment figures, as Bowlby, Winnicott and others have shown.

If most mothers are "good enough", some are not so good and some are too good. As Neumann states (1973): "The effects of too much or too little attention to the child are equally negative" (p. 21). It is the same with fathers whose function is to lay down the law and which we have already considered in our chapter on Lacan. It is better to have a strict father than a father who is too nice and so ineffectual, as in the case of Little Hans's father who failed to castrate his child, to put it in Lacanian terminology. A not so good mother fails to satisfy her children's needs. A too good mother stifles her child by constantly fulfilling such needs and stunting the child's individuality and independence. She suffocates him with her love and the father, in such cases, must intervene and speak his "No". Of course, as Klein recognised, a good (personal) mother may be perceived of as a terrible one through no fault of her own. What matters is not the actual behaviour, good or otherwise, of the mother but, as Bowlby suggested, the archetypal experience actualised by her in the child. As both Bowlby and Lacan recognise, a critical factor in the aetiology of psychopathology is not the actual mother or father, but the mother and father complex which is formed in the subject's psyche.

From this *participation mystique* (of mother and child), to use a

Jungian expression, the child's ego becomes differentiated. The ego, understood by Jung as the conscious part of the personality, emerges from the Self. As Jung writes: "The ego stands to the Self as the moved to the mover ... the Self ... is an *a priori* existent out of which the ego evolves. It is, so to speak, an unconscious prefiguration of the ego" (*CW* 11, para. 391). This is the ego-Self axis. The child's ego consciousness will gradually grow and he will begin to recognise his parents as separate subjects possessing a desire of their own just as he must recognise his own desire. Good-enough mothering allows the child to achieve basic-trust in Erikson's sense. The mother–child relationship is, in short, the primal one from which all other attachments evolve.

Signs of illness emerge early on. There is, as we have been continually saying and stressing, an association between maternal deficiency especially, institutional care and the later penchant for criminality. Ethological studies have shown that similar abnormalities appear in offspring whose bonding to mother has been stunted or impaired. Of course, the loss may not involve the *biological* mother. What matters is the primary care giver who consistently and over a long period provides maternal care to the child. Premature puncturing of this primary relationship may lead to serious pathology in subsequent years. As Bowlby has demonstrated in a study of children aged between 15 and 30 months of age (1969), the duration of the separation or loss is related to the degree of the damage caused. In short, the earlier and longer the separation or loss is, the worse it is.

The father's function is also crucial, a fact to which both Jung and Lacan have attested. The father plays a crucial role in "the destiny of the individual", as Jung outlined in his 1909 paper entitled "The Significance of the Father in the Destiny of the Individual" (*CW* 4). In this paper and in later additions, Jung stresses the personal father as well as the father archetype. According to Jung, the father is the opposite to the mother in that he incorporates different attributes and attitudes; he is an "informing spirit" (*CW* 5, para. 70), a representative of the spiritual principle and personal counterpart of God the Father, a model persona for his son and the first lover and animus figure for his daughter. Lacan, as we have shown in chapter five, stresses the vital importance of the name-of-the-father in the life of the subject. He is not alone, however. Van der Heydt (1973) comments that psychology as a whole has over-emphasised the personal mother. Klein and the Kleinians have been the most guilty in this regard it has to be said. Like Lacan, Seligman (1982) bemoans the fact of the "missing father" and she asks whether the father is in reality excluded or whether he excludes himself. Blomeyer expresses a cultural concern in this age of manifest matriarchy (1982). Carvalho (1982) enumerates the ways in which the father can facilitate the psychological development of the infant. The father's function is vital in the formation of the child's sense of generational and gender identity. Samuels (1982), for his part, stresses the infant's ability to discern mother and father as separate entities. Jung describes the importance of the father, the fact that parental psychology and psychopathology can influence the child and that the child's personality can likewise influence the parents (*CW* 4, paras. 91–92). Like the psychoanalysts, Jung acknowledges the Oedipus complex as an archetypally determined phase of development but rejected the idea that coitus was desired. Jung thought that incest was not literally sexual but symbolic (*CW* 5), but he did recognise that sexuality plays a part and stressed the whole life-cycle, pre-empting Levinson (1978), Erikson (1951), Maduro and Wheelwright (1977), Staude (1981) and a whole host of others in the field of adult life-span developmental psychology (see Jung "The Stages of Life", *CW* 8).

In relation to the personal and archetypal father, Jung writes: "The personal father inevitably embodies the archetype, which is what endows this figure with its fascinating power. The archetype acts as an amplifier, enhancing beyond measure the effects that proceed from the father, so far as these conform to the inherited pattern" (*CW* 4, para. 744). In mythology, legends, dreams and fairytales, the father archetype is personified by the King, the Lawgiver, the Father in Heaven and, like the mother, has a dual aspect, incorporating both positive and negative features. He is the Terrible Father, Shiva, Kronos who devours his children. Most analysts agree that the father archetype is constellated at a later stage, ontologically, than the mother archetype; this was also noted by Aristotle in his books on friendship in the *Nicomachean Ethics*. The father's function differs from the mother's. The dynamics involved have been brilliantly delineated by Lacan, as we outlined in chapter five. The father's function facilitates the transition of the child from centripetal concerns to centrifugal concerns, from the Imaginary to the Symbolic order. Furthermore, the child's relationship with mother is confirmed and consolidated through the bond with its father. The child must disengage from the mother and father and struggle to be recognised outside the family group or else he goes to his death without having achieved a personality of his own, as Hegel and Lacan stress. Lacan notes: "In the area of personal dignity, the family can only promote the individual to being an entity who is named, and it can only do this at the hour of his burial" (1938, p. 12).

Although we have already covered the Oedipus complex in earlier chapters, I would like to make a few points on its relevance and revelatory character in the structure of the family in which the subject grows up and in which can be gleaned the eternal entity of desire.

We have mentioned the "weaning complex", but the early Lacan also mentions the "intrusion complex" where the subject realises he has siblings who appear to him as usurpers. Such dynastic positions disrupt the effects of fraternity and introduce jealousy, which Lacan describes as an "archetypal sentiment" (1938, p. 13). Because jealous love manifests itself as hatred, it sets up aggressivity, like the mirror stage before it. Lacan observes: "The intrusion originates from the newcomer and infects the occupant. In general, this occurs in a family with a birth and in principle it is the elder child who suffers" (p. 24). The Oedipus complex, then, is concerned with many of these psychic relationships and as the nodal complex of neuroses, it defines psychic relationships within the family and constellates sexual desire. Family events and family constellations determine symptoms and structures and are, thus, paramount. In the family, one can observe domestic tyranny, sentimental demands, masculine protest (of women who hold on to the purse strings), castrating fathers or fathers who are lacking (as all fathers are), "whether absent or humiliated, divided or sham" (Lacan, ibid. p. 45). Discord between the parental couple is another important factor. Lacan notes:

> There is the mother who smothers the children and indulges in excesses of tenderness which express, more or less consciously, repressed impulses; or the paradoxically dried-up mother full of unspoken severity and unconscious cruelty which express an

altogether more profound fixation of the libido ... This is why a lack of harmony between the parents is always harmful to the child and why the secret forms of discord are even more pernicious than the memories of the squabbles of which he is conscious [ibid., p. 71].

In the family, finally, there can be witnessed the harmony and Heraclitean strife of married life which makes it "a privileged place for the cultivation of neuroses"! (Lacan, ibid. p. 73).

So we can see how the early years are absolutely paramount for the child's mental health and happiness. Psychopathology ensues when the natural consequences and configurations of the child's archetypal programme are frustrated rather than fulfilled. It is this "frustration of archetypal intent", to use Stevens's expression, that we must now examine before applying the insights gained thus far to what the evolutionary psychiatrists also call the "antisocial personality disorder".

The frustration of archetypal intent

In neurotics, there is a history of dysfunctional family dynamics, of deficient parental care, such as parental abuse, separation, loss, unresponsiveness, induction of guilt etc., which frustrates the archetypal intent and the imperatives inherent in the maturing Self. Such pathogenic parenting inevitably leads to pathology. Two adages by Oscar Wilde contain, in this regard, pertinent psychological wisdom: "All women become like their mothers. That is their tragedy. No man does. That is his." and "Children begin by loving their parents. As they grow older they judge them. Sometimes they forgive them". Though the child's archetypal potential may be thwarted by the parents, it persists and remains ever active in the unconscious, demanding realisation in reality. For example, to put this in Jungian terms, absence (either physical or psychical) or masculine deficiency on the part of the father will fail to activate the father archetype within the male subject's psyche, with the result that the boy's masculine principle will remain unactivated and he will be left to languish under the dominance of the mother complex. Failure to be present on both fronts, physically and psychically, can result in gross pathology. The consequences of growing up without a mother and a father (contrary to the Imaginary musings of the militant feminists) can be catastrophic indeed. Such a suitable "rearing environment", as Bowlby puts it, involves one male and one female caring for the child. This is the optimal model. The more the family deviates from this, the more probable it is that the child will develop atypically. So children being reared in orphanages would tend to show some developmental disturbances, those growing up in single-parent families might be slightly better off but some form of atypical maturation might occur, while children growing up in borstals and penal institutions would be the most serious category and could easily develop into an "antisocial personality disorder". The best hope is for children to develop in a stable and loving two parent family environment. All the recent sociological statistics point to the stunted moral, emotional and cognitive growth of individuals reared without fathers due to separation, desertion or divorce. In the US more than 10% of all children (eight million persons) live in fatherless families (Herzog and Sudia, 1970). Sometimes the figure is as high as 50%. Increasingly, children are being brought up by substitute carers.

When such archetypal imperatives are stunted or repressed, these archetypal components can erupt in a more drastic and primitive fashion. To give an example, Jung believed that the father archetype in the German collective unconscious was contaminated by the Teutonic myth of Wotan, which we mentioned briefly in chapter two. And Hitler, according to Jung, was in the grip of repressed Wotanic aspects. Jung opines: "The impressive thing about the German phenomena is that one man, who is obviously "possessed", has infected a whole nation to such an extent that everything is set in motion and has started rolling on its course towards perdition" (CW 10, para. 388). In the same paper (1936), Jung outlines what may be awaiting reactivation in the unconscious:

> It was not in Wotan's nature to linger on and show signs of old age. He simply disappeared when the times turned against him, and remained invisible for more than a thousand years, working anonymously and indirectly. Archetypes are like river beds which dry up when the water deserts them, but which it can find again at any time. An archetype is like an old water-course along which the water of life has flowed in this channel the more likely it is that sooner or later the water will return to its old bed. The life of the individual as a member of society and particularly of the State may

be regulated like a canal, but the life of nations is a great rushing river which is utterly beyond human controls ... Thus the life of nations rolls on unchecked, without guidance, unconscious of where it is going, like a rock crashing down the side of a hill, until it is stopped by an obstacle stronger than itself. Political events move from one impasse to the next, like a torrent caught in gullies, creeks and marshes. All human control comes to an end when the individual is caught in a mass movement. Then the archetypes begin to function, as happens also in the lives of individuals when they are confronted with situations that cannot be dealt with in any of the familiar ways [CW 10, para. 395].

Obviously, this negativity can erupt in far less drastic a manner in the individual subject when his archetypal bioprogramme is frustrated by familial configurations, particularly implicating the mother. As Neumann states (1973, p. 41): "A child's later personal relationship to its mother, as the basis for every subsequent love relationship and indeed of every human relationship, stands or falls with the primal relationship". It can lead to myriad manifestations of psychopathology, ranging from hysteria to obsessional neurosis, from phobias and perversions to criminality, thus perpetuating an unending cycle. As Bowlby says: "each of us is apt to do unto others as we have been done by. The bullying adult is the bullied child grown bigger" (1979, p. 141).

According to the Jungians, the child must be able to explore the environment and actualise the Self's potential, both of which require aggression. Parents need to be able to tolerate and accept rather than frustrate the expression of their child's aggression so that it can become assimilated and integrated into the conscious personality. As Stevens outlines (1982, p. 134), several possiblities arise in relation to aggression: (1) it can be turned inwards and directed towards the Self leading to self-loathing; (2) it can be displaced on to a scapegoat (racial minorities, homosexuals etc.); (3) it can be transformed into idealisation of the aggressor; and (4) it can be eroticised as in sadism and masochism.

In summary we can state with Stevens that: (1) parental complexes and personal parents can create the conditions for the constellation of archetypal forces and processes and the formation of complexes; (2) many complex interacting dynamics can lead to either frustration or fulfilment of archetypal imperatives to a lesser or greater degree; and (3) be responsible for human psychopathology. Criminality can't be said to have one, single cause; not poverty, violent videos or television programmes (as the Home Office recently concluded). It is a complex constellation and confluence of constitutional factors (innate structures), familial environment and environmental forces all interacting and competing with one another in dynamic and dialectical interplay.

Evolutionary psychiatry again

Before applying the perspective of evolutionary psychiatry to the "antisocial personality disorder", it is necessary to outline its main principles and propositions. To this end, the book entitled *Evolutionary Psychiatry* by Stevens and Price will be our guide in this dense and difficult domain. So what exactly is evolutionary psychiatry?

Darwin suggested that we have evolved through the process of natural selection and genetic mutation and he showed that all species are interrelated. In common with other animal species, our innate predisposition and propensities (the human genome) are dependent on environmental variables for their expression. The archetypal programme with which we are endowed is adapted to enable us to survive in the environment in which we have evolved. There is no great need or reason for me to enter into the delicate intricacies of evolutionary theory. A summary of the major points of this discipline will suffice.

According to the ethological and evolutionary viewpoint, we possess an ontogenetic aspect, which proceeds and develops on the basis of a phylogenetic blueprint. This view opposes the *tabula rasa* or blank slate model, which has been adopted by behaviourism, and is in accord with Jung's archetypal hypothesis, which we have just been considering. If Jung predated this viewpoint, it was Bowlby who first introduced ethological insights into psychiatry and depth-psychology and postulated the existence of innate predisposing behavioural structures and characteristics.

In Waddington's words (1957), epigenetic pathways exist along which ontogenesis proceeds. This corresponds to Jung's concept of the Self, employed to designate the totality of the psyche, the sum total of archetypal potential. The archetypes of the phylogenetic psyche are actualised in the normal or pathological complexes of the ontogenetic psyche, as Jung has shown. The maturational process, as Winnicott calls it, proceeds through a sequence of innate expectations, imperatives and archetypal anticipations, which the environment fulfils or frustrates. In this respect, the family, as a universal, biological, archetypal configuration, is so fundamental in the production of "normal" developmental psychology and "abnormal" human psychopathology.

The ethological and evolutionary perspective represents a rediscovery of Jung's archetypal theory. As Stevens and Price sum up: "It is as if each of us were a travelling orchestra with a number of well-rehearsed symphonies and concertos in our repertoire from which we select, for each performance, the programme we consider most appropriate for the audience, the venue, and the fee (that is, the pay off in terms of cost/benefit)" (1996, p. 26). In short, our archetypal propensities pervade our social roles, our biosocial goals and our behavioural systems. Frustration of archetypal expectations leads to various forms of pathology. Stevens and Price cite two interesting examples to support the above contention. In 1925 the authorities in London Zoo placed one hundred hamadryas baboons in a concrete mound surrounded by a moat, known as Monkey Hill. It was supposed to have been an all-male population but six females were accidentally included. Violent battles and vicious struggles ensued and within two years, 44 of them were dead. Then the authorities put 30 more females on the island. Within a month, 15 females had been butchered. What happened? Ethological observation showed that out of captivity hamadryas baboons live peaceful, well-ordered lives. But the behaviour of these baboons was abnormal. The most obvious explanation is that within the rigid confines and constraining circumstances in which the zoo authorities compelled them to live, this constituted a gross frustration of their archetypal needs. Monkey Hill supplied the creatures with 540 m^2. However, a troop of 100 baboons would normally need a range of 50,000 m^2—nearly 100 times the size. The reason that psychopathic savagery resulted was due to the different wild troops being assembled and crowded into tiny areas where there are more males than females. "Frustration of archetypal intent" caused by the zoo environment led to harrowing psychopathology.

Similar happenings occur to human beings when deprived of

their archetypal needs. Indeed many of us live in an urban habitat which Desmond Morris labelled the "human zoo". The second example cited is a story about the IK, a group of hunter-gatherers from Uganda who were driven from their range of 40,000 km^2, placed in shack settlements and instructed in subsistence farming. Within a short space of time, they became depressed, demoralised, anxious and ill and behaved with psychopathic indifference to all and sundry including their spouses and children. Similar break-down into a sequelae of suicide, alcoholism and depression can be observed in the Aboriginal culture of Australia and the Amerindian one in the US (see ibid. p. 31).

Stevens's and Price's model for mental health and illness is provided by this perspective and stated in the following terms: "mental health depends upon the provision of physical and social environments capable of meeting the archetypal needs of the developing individual; psychopathology can result when these needs are frustrated" (ibid.). Their basic principle of psychopathol-ogy has already been stated, that "psychopathology results when the environment fails, either partially or totally, to meet one or more of these archetypal needs in the developing individual", a premise originally adumbrated by John Bowlby. What then are these archetypal needs and what environments are able to guarantee their fulfilment?

Our ancestors lived in small communities consisting of about 40–50 individuals as Fox, an anthropologist, has deduced from ethnographic accounts (1989). Our large sprawling anonymous modern urban environments, our lack of community-based kinship bonds, the disruption of families through separation and the social evil of divorce, the alarming and increasing incidence of one-parent families, the lack of intimate care of children as mothers remain at work, the lack of contact with nature and the loss of myth, ritual and religion in many people's lives, together with a whole host of modern phenomena ranging from mortgage rate increases, house prices, morally unacceptable levels of high taxation, sexual abuse and rising crime statistics are all connected with Western society's failure to satisfy certain archetypal needs (see Glantz and Pearce, 1989). As Jung observed, modern urban life breeds "disalliance with the unconscious [which] is synonymous with loss of instinct and rootlessness" (CW 7, para. 195). Similar points were made by

Nietzsche and developed by Freud in his *Civilization and Its Discontents* (1930) and by Jung in *Modern Man in Search of a Soul* (1933).

Stevens and Price, in the light of this research, posit five laws of *psycho*dynamics which they enumerate as follows:

1. Whenever a phenomenon is found to be characteristic of all human communities, irrespective of culture, race or historical epoch, then it is an expression of an innate property or archetype.
2. Archetypes possess an inherent dynamic whose goal is to actualise themselves in both psyche and behaviour.
3. Mental health results from the fulfilment of archetypal goals.
4. Psychopathology results from the frustration of archetypal goals.
5. Psychiatric symptoms are persistent exaggerations of adaptive psychophysiological responses [ibid. p. 38].

Thus, as Aristotle recognised, the acorn will become an oak tree, the caterpillar a butterfly, given the right kind of soil, the condition of climate etc. Nature decrees that acorns become oak trees and caterpillars become butterflies. So an acorn is and is not an oak tree. An acorn is *potentially* an oak tree and an oak tree is an *actualised* acorn. Change or becoming resides in the transition from potential being (potency) to actual being (act). This is the metaphysical equivalent of Jung's psychological notion of individuation, in which we actualise or realise our potentialities, becoming, in some sense, what we are already because we cannot become what we are not. Frustration of this archetypal intent in the acorn or caterpillar can lead to stunted growth, disease or death.

The cause of a number of psychopathological conditions, according to this evolutionary perspective, is due to competition for two valued resources: *attachment* and *rank*. Bowlby brought attachment into the ambit of psychiatry. He demonstrated not only that attachment is instinctive, but that it is designed to maintain physical proximity and social communication between bonded partners (parents or otherwise). The consequences of the disruption of this bond formation, especially in early childhood, can have devastating results, as Winnicott has also shown. Stable attachment is associated with emotional security, health and well being and the adoption of a coherent and cohesive sense of self. A flawed self-concept can lead to *anxious attachment* (Bowlby), depression and detachment. In Bowlby's formulation, the mother (or mother substitute) provides a *secure base* for the child, or an emotional *container*, in Bion's words. All analytic schools (and common-sense) agree that the best start in life is to be born to parents who love and trust and care for one another and their children. Developmental psychology has shown that children who grow up in stable families (relatively speaking!) are more likely to enjoy mental health and be relatively free from neurotic symptoms. Such children possess a "strong ego", in the language of the ego-psychologists; they have "introjected a good breast", as the Kleinians would say; have been "successfully castrated" according to the Lacanians; have established "basic trust", in Erikson's terms; have displayed "mature dependence", for Fairbairn. Bowlby would consider that they possess a "secure base" and in Jungian terms, they are on the road to "individuation".

Neurotic illness, on the other hand, occurs when such archetypal needs, as we have been saying, are frustrated. In particular, where there is deficient parental care displayed, then the attachment bonds cannot be properly or securely formed, basic loving trust firmly established, or the superego (Jung's "moral complex") cogently constructed. Of all these archetypal imperatives, the one that needs most consolidating is the mother–child bond; this is absolutely indispensable. Proper maternal care is as necessary for physical health as vitamin D is for the development of bones, as Bowlby noted (1951). Bowlby also demonstrated that many children who were reared in institutions where love was not apparent or made manifest grew up retarded, physically, socially, intellectually and emotionally. So many theorists, especially Bowlby and Winnicott, have alerted us to the link between institutional care, maternal deprivation and the subsequent development of a "sociopathic" personality structure. Bowlby charts *three* stages in which separated children predictably pass: *protest, despair* and *detachment*. Furthermore, such separation can affect the personality structure for life. When, due to maternal deprivation, the child is incapable of eliciting care, it enters into a state of "anxious attachment", becoming prey to neurotic anxiety. Each stage of separation relates to core and central psychoanalytic states: protest relates to *separation anxiety*, despair to *depression* and detachment to *schizoid personality disorder*. Moreover, under parental influence, the child gradually acquires his own version of the moral code, which Freud called the superego and Jung labelled the moral complex. For Freud, the superego emerges at the resolution of the Oedipus complex as a result or response to the fear of being castrated.

The formation and maintenance of warm, enduring and intimate bonds in infancy and childhood is absolutely crucial in order to minimise potential pathology. Needless to say, actual physical contact such as stroking, holding or cuddling by the primary care giver in the early years is a major component of attachment formation not only in terms of the child's emotional stability but also for sexual development. Pathogenic parenting results from parental absence or separation from the child (the earlier and longer the loss, the more severe the consequences), parental unresponsiveness, parental threats of abandonment, parental induction of inferiority feelings and neurotic clinging to the child, usually by the mother (see Stevens and Price, 1996, p. 45). As Lacan stated, in such cases the father's function is to castrate the mother and stop the mother–child bond from being or becoming too suffocating. That said, "good enough mothering" will probably produce "good enough" children and "good enough" (non-criminal) adult subjects.

Evolutionary psychiatry and antisocial personality disorder

Now that we have outlined the main principles and propositions of evolutionary psychiatry, we can see how they apply to the "antisocial personality disorder". There is substantial agreement between the classificatory system of nosological entities in the *American DSM-IV* compared with the *European ICD 10*. Both agree that when talking of what constitutes "personality disorders", (in their language), they are referring to the sum total of cognitive, emotional and behavioural repertoires or characteristics which the human subject habitually employs in relating to his environment or *Umwelt*, and which persist over time and constitute a fundamental aspect of the human subject's usual functioning. Both also concur that "personality disorders" have their onset in childhood and adolescence.

There are ten "personality disorders" outlined in *DSM IV*. From the point of view of evolutionary psychiatry, Stevens and Price classify five of these "disorders"—"antisocial", "histrionic", "narcissistic", "dependent" and "obsessive–compulsive" personality disorders—as being "disorders" of *attachment* and *rank*. They also include "type A personality disorder" in this schema. They classify *"borderline"* and *"schizotypal* personality disorders" as *borderline states* while "paranoid", "schizoid" and "avoidant personality disorders" are classified as *spacing disorders*. Following Harpending and Sobus (1987), they argue that there is a genetic link between the "antisocial personality disorder" and the "hysterical personality disorder".

We have already had occasion to dwell on attachment theory but what exactly is rank-theory? Evolutionary psychiatrists argue that in our phylogenetic history, which unfolded over millions of years, there was a history of ancestral competitiveness for social rank and resources such as food, territory and mates. Once rank was acquired, access to resources was made available. This competition for rank was evident in the various threat displays and physical combat contests, which ethologists refer to as *ritual agonistic behaviour* (RAB). Success in such contests provided a measure of the subject's *resource holding power* (RHP). Two forms of defensive behaviour ensue when the animal is threatened: submission or escape. The human equivalent of resource holding power is self-esteem.

On a related theme: Michael Chance (Chance and Jolly, 1970), in the course of observing social groups of primates, recognised two modes of functioning which he termed the *agonic* and the *hedonic*. The agonic mode operates in hierarchically constructed societies where individuals are concerned with warding off threats to their status and inhibiting overt expression of aggression. In other words, the potential for violence and agonistic aggression is present but inhibited. The hedonic mode operates in more egalitarian societies where affiliative behaviour is the norm and organic conflict absent. As Stevens and Price (1996) recognise, these two forms of social organisation find historical parallels in the Empedoclean distinction between love and strife, from which Freud derives his later dualistic instinct theory of Eros and Thanatos, and Aristotle's distinction between the political and the hedonic life. Thus, there seem to be two archetypal systems present; one concerned with attachment, affiliation and altruism and the other one concerned with rank, status, territory and possessions and, of course, law and order.

For Stevens and Price, "antisocial and histrionic personality disorder" represents a "disorder of attachment and rank". In delineating the nosology and phenomenology of "antisocial personality disorder", these authors deviate little from that described in *DSM IV*. They maintain that the social strategy residing at the core of both disorders is *deceit*. Those individuals with "antisocial personality disorder" violate others and disregard the subsequent risk to their safety, fail to conform to lawful behaviour, lie, use aliases, con others, are impulsive, irritable and aggressive, are frequently arrested and charged with assault, are socially mobile, display a lack of remorse and rationalise their actions. They tend to have a history of impulsiveness, hyperactivity, delinquency and aggressive sexual activity. Though they can be charming and possess charisma and sex appeal, they are manipulative and tend not to form lasting emotional bonds. Males are 20 times more likely to be categorised as suffering from "antisocial personality disorder" than females. In the latter, however, there is a much higher incidence of "hysterical personality disorder".

"Hysterical" or "histrionic personality disorder" is characterised by behavioural patterns of attention seeking, self-dramatisation, theatrical posturing, exaggerated behaviour, inappropriate seductive sexual behaviour. They engage in over-emphatic forms of speech and dress, claim closer relationships with socially or sexually desirable people than is the case and tend to be highly impressionable. They tend to have dramatic medical histories and manifest occasional conversion symptoms (psychosomatic signs and symptoms). Like "psychopaths", they often engage in promiscuous sexual activity. Furthermore, a high incidence of "histrionic personality disorder" can be found among the female prison population (see Stevens and Price, 1996, p. 84).

As to their aetiology, all "personality disorders" (so-called) are a combination of genetic and early environmental factors. In our chapters on Winnicott and Klein and from the observations carried out by Bowlby, we have an idea of what these environmental influences might be. In relation to genetic factors, it has been found that the children of "psychopathic" patients are more likely to be characterised as possessing "antisocial personality disorder" than the children of parents who possess different types of personality structure, even when such children are adopted. Also, identical twins have a concordance rate of 60% for criminal behaviour as distinct from dizygotic twins who possess a rate of 15%. Stevens and Price make the point: "Although criminal behaviour is not synonymous with psychopathy, the high proportion of psychopaths in the prison population suggests that the high concordance for criminality may reflect the concordance for antisocial personality disorder" (1996, p. 85). In other words, not all criminals are psychopaths, but most (if not all) psychopaths are criminals. A psychopath is *not* a psychotic but a psychotic who commits criminal acts, in other words, a psychotic criminal. From a Lacanian perspective, I would like to label, what psychiatry calls a "psychopath", a psychotic (or 'rosy') criminal—a case of being mad rather than bad.

In relation to psychodynamic factors, "psychopaths" have failed to form a mature superego which, as we have said, is dependent on emotional bonding and intimate, warm, loving and lasting relationships with parental objects. The majority of "psychopaths" provide a history of parental separation, loss, disharmony, absence and institutional care. In relation to neurophysiology, there does appear to be some abnormalities in the autonomous and central nervous system. EEG studies have shown such neurophysiological anomalies present in approximately 50% of individuals examined. Together with the psycho-galvanic skin response, these prove that in "psychopathic" patients, there is a chronic under-arousal of the autonomic nervous system which means that "psychopaths" have a higher threshold for the experience of fear and anxiety than non-"psychopaths" who achieve a higher pulse rate in stressful situations and engage in dangerous, stimulus-seeking behaviour "just for the fun of it". As Mednick and Christiansen (1977) have shown, it is relatively easy for "psychopaths" to engage in antisocial acts as they experience little fear or anxiety.

From the evolutionary perspective and "ranking" psychology, according to Stevens and Price, both the "psychopath" and the hysteric are *free riders*. Free-riders are "individuals who seek to divert to themselves an undue proportion of the group's resources without first satisfying the usual requirements of achieving high social rank" (ibid. p. 86). The American anthropologists, Axelrod and Hamilton (1981), and Harpending and Sobus (1987), maintain that both "psychopathy" and hysteria are adaptive strategies and argue that, due to the different reproductive strategies of males and females, each will exhibit different patterns of cheating. The male might persuade the female to copulate with him by deceiving her about his degree of commitment and resources. The female cheater may feign a lack of interest in copulation so as to lure or lull the male into a false sense of security as to his paternity of the offspring that might emerge from such an amorous encounter. She may also exaggerate the need for a strong male and display her feminine helplessness and vulnerability. According to Stevens and Price, these descriptions fit the clinical data for "psychopathy" in males and hysteria in females. They observe: "Psychopaths are indeed highly mobile, charming and charismatic, sexually hyperactive non-reciprocators. Hysterics are fecund reproducers, who are skilled at exaggerating their needs, especially to males" (ibid. p. 87). For these authors, both "psychopathy" and hysteria are part genetically transmitted, with hysteria in females and "psychopathy" in males both being the outcome of the *same* genetic material. Hysteria is thus seen, in this light, as representing a mild form of "psychopathy".

There is much interesting material in the above accounts. But to describe "psychopaths" as free-riders and to describe their structure solely in terms of orthodox and evolutionary *psychiatry* pays little attention to unconscious, psychoanalytic factors, and cannot therefore be wholly convincing or illuminating. Before proceeding to critique this medical model of mind from a Lacanian perspective, I will summarise the biological and sociological findings of psychiatry in relation to the "antisocial personality disorder". We can say that *some* of the following features *may* figure in the *environment* of the potential criminal in whom natural archetypal imperatives have been grossly frustrated:

1. prolonged separation from or loss of mother and/or father (emotional deprivation);
2. pathogenic parenting;
3. history of violence in the family;
4. history of alcohol and/or drugs misuse;
5. history of sexual abuse; and
6. institutionalised care and/or homelessness.

The criminal will tend to be:

1. single, young and male;
2. psychologically and morally immature and egocentric;
3. impulsive;
4. deceitful and manipulative;
5. solipsistic;
6. a free-rider;
7. narcissistic;
8. borderline;
9. histrionic;
10. equipped with an underdeveloped capacity for concern, and hence, unrepentant and lacking in (imaginative) identification with others (viz., empathic);
11. socially deprived and/or alienated; and
12. biologically, there may be some neurophysiological abnormalities present.

We can see from the above that there are indeed social and biological factors predisposing a subject to criminality but important as these aspects undoubtedly are, the psychiatric model does not take cognisance of *unconscious* concomitants, which are the primary foci of this research. So it seems pertinent at this juncture to pose some criticisms of the psychiatric/medical model of mind before offering a synthesis of the *psychoanalytic* factors involved in the following and final chapter.

Lacan's discourse of the master: a critique of the psychiatric model

Psychiatry represents a movement away from the consideration of *unconscious* configurations, which are the proper concern of psychoanalysis. In psychiatry, the unconscious becomes eclipsed, elided. With all its talk of "disorder" (as if there is a "norm") and "diagnosable diseases", psychiatry reduces the suffering subject to his symptoms and pays no attention to his *structure*. Lacanian psychoanalysis conceptualises *three* structures, as we outlined in the introduction—neurosis, psychosis and perversion. One is neurotic, psychotic or perverse. One can therefore be a neurotic, psychotic or perverse criminal, a neurotic, psychotic or perverse homosexual, a neurotic, psychotic or perverse heterosexual etc. In such a schemata, there can be *three* and only *three* structures, in *one* of which we are inscribed as subjects. There are, thus, no "borderlines" and no "personality disorders". Furthermore, psychiatry is, in Lacan's terms, a Master discourse. In Lacan's clinical theorising, there are *four* discourses—the discourse of the master, university discourse, analytic discourse and the hysteric's discourse (Lacan was one himself!). His theory of the four discourses will not be discussed in detail as it would take us too far afield but, by way of critique, let my briefly mention the scientific discourse of the master which belongs to the psychiatrist, among others.

The discourse of the master includes all those subjects who deny their structural lack, that is, they deny the fact of their own division. They are all-knowing subjects who cannot not know. Their knowledge is totalising and complete, without gaps, holes, fissures or rifts. It is like the discourse of the university with its accumulated knowledge. Both radically oppose the discourse of the analyst, which brings unconscious knowledge to the place of truth. The discourse of the master, in our case the psychiatrist, is a black and white discourse where there are no shades of grey. It is univocal because scientific. At least, that is their phantasy. Its language is clear and concise; it is to do with measurement, verification and falsification. It dislikes theory, concerning itself solely with praxis. Certain questions are not answered or even asked—questions concerning the subject of the unconscious and truth as cause. Of these subjects, they want to know nothing. There may be a passion for knowledge but not for truth. The divided, split subject occupies the place of truth, through whom the big Other (the unconscious) will, from time to time, speak.

Scientific and psychiatric discourse represses the cause of the divided subject's desire, known in Lacanian terminology, as the *objet petit a*. The Real, which is always in evidence in psychiatry, clinical psychology, even counselling (in the Clinic in other words), is shunned, shut out. It has no place and is silenced. Psychiatry separates the subject from his disease and it is the latter which will be "tested" and "treated", usually with pharmacological pills ("a pill for every ill").

The master (psychiatrist) will not face up to the truth of his own unconscious, which is barred, barricaded. The failure of the relationship between master/psychiatrist and patient/subject will be concealed, covered up even, by the constant accumulation of knowledge in terms of facts, files, test-material, data-collecting and correlating etc. Eventually, the suffering subject will be commanded to undergo treatment and soon becomes an object for the Other. The psychiatrist (who is not obliged to undergo any form of analysis or therapy as part of his training) proudly proclaims: "I am master of myself" ("maître/m'être à moi-même"). Medical discourse is an example of the discourse of the master, *par excellence*. It is a classic case.

The psychiatrist is supposed to know everything. He is a *"sujet supposé savoir"* but there is a *savoir sans sujet*—the Unconscious. The knowledge of the psychiatrist is absolute, Hegelian. As such, it opposes the doctrine of divine ignorance, which the figure of wise Socrates of old embodied. Socrates showed up the Sophists for the men they were, men who knew everything that was to be known, men who, therefore, knew nothing about the unconscious, about truth, or about desire. These were the only things Socrates knew, apart from knowing that the Delphic oracle had described him as the wisest man because he knew that he did not know everything. But was that not enough to know?

Unlike Socrates, the psychiatrist will not doubt, will never utter Descartes' words: *"Dubito, ergo sum"*, because where there is doubt, hesitancy, uncertainty, lack, there is, assuredly, the subject of the Unconscious which is the only (psychological) Truth.

CHAPTER SEVEN

Towards a synthesis

"[Gary] Gilmore brought the Automatic to Jensen's head. 'This one is for me', he said and fired. 'This one is for Nicole', he said and fired again. The body reacted each time. He stood up. There was a lot of blood. It spread across the floor at a surprising rate. Some of it got into the bottom of his pants. He walked out of the rest room with the bills in his pocket, the coin changer in his hand, walked by the big Coke machine and the phone on the wall, walked out of this real clean gas station ... Around nine o'clock he started to go back to Spanish Fork to look for Nicole, but on the way he stopped at a store ... In the middle of washing the couch cushions, Debbie Bushnell went out to the front office and asked Ben to go to the store and get some low-fat milk ... Then she heard Ben talking to somebody in the front office. She thought maybe there was a child there, because she heard a balloon pop. So she went out to talk ... Ben was on the floor. He just lay there face down, and his legs were shaking. When she bent over to look at him, she saw his head was bleeding ... A wave of blood kept rising out of his hair. She put her hand on it. She sat there with the phone in her free hand ringing the operator ... She couldn't tell how long before help came"

Norman Mailer, *The Executioner's Song*

Psychiatry, biology, sociology and law can lure us away from looking at the subject in relation to his structure. They represent, as we said in the last chapter, movements away from the unconscious. I am only able to engage and employ an analytic discourse whose theory informs and guides one's practice. Of psychiatry, biology, sociology and law, to name a few, I can say very little and, to paraphrase Wittgenstein, must pass over in silence. Such are my limits and the limitations imposed, necessarily, on this book. Though, of course, these other discourses are important in highlighting significant social, biological, behavioural and legal aspects of criminality, they can hide the subject and what we have offered in this work is a theory of the subject, of the pale criminal subject in relation to his structure. Such a theory of the subject enables practical application in that what one has to say theoretically is relevant practically. Dialectically speaking, the analytic discipline incorporates *teoria* and *praxis*. One informs the other. And as Lacan said: "la psychanalyse, c'est la science du particulier". In this final chapter, I wish to offer a dialectical synthesis of the psychoanalytic perspectives on pale criminality I have been developing.

Dialectics

Dialectics is associated with the name of G.W.F. Hegel, the 19th century German idealist philosopher. Philosophically, dialectics evolves in a threefold structure thus: thesis (affirmation or assertion), antithesis (negation or annulment) and synthesis (reconciliation of opposites or transcendence). This dialectical system unfolds in a tripartite manner from a construction through a deconstruction towards a reconstruction. In Hegelian metaphysics, all life proceeds and progresses dialectically. The erroneous idealist and rationalist intricacies of Hegel's absolutising system need not detain us here. Its methodology, however, is useful and can be utilised and applied to our concerns in the province of psychoanalysis.

But before Hegel and Marx, Plato employed dialectics in the *Republic*, maintaining that no one person possesses the truth. The truth emerges as a function of the conversation between the various parties re: the nature of justice. It is in this dialogical process that truth emerges—it is not the property of one single individual. By way of illustration Plato uses the metaphor of the sticks. Imagine rubbing a number of sticks together, the question is: which stick produced the fire? The fire is not reducible to any one stick.

Jung provided the psychological equivalent of Hegel's "synthesis", terming it the "transcendent function", which designates the mutual interaction and influence exerted between the ego and the Self in the course of individuation.

Lacan, who was heavily influenced by Hegel, maintained that psychoanalysis was essentially a dialectical operation. I think one could say that the patient's conscious discourse (the Empty Word) is deconstructed by the analyst/dialectician through analytic interpretation and insight (or even, and especially, through silence), while, at times, allowing for a radical reconstruction by the patient of his Real life experiences and events. In the frustration of the silences, in the parapraxes, dreams and in the symptoms of the subject, the big Other of the unconscious erupts and the Full Word is spoken. Unconscious discourse (which speaks us) operates by way of the second moment in dialectics, subverting the conscious *cogito* of the subject. The movement of psychoanalysis is by way of a dialectical transvaluation and transmogrification. Synthesis, the third realisation, born between patient and analyst, conscious and unconscious intentions, thesis and antithesis, occurs in the sacred space of the analyst's consulting room where analytic *praxis* alone bears fruit and yields endless possibilities. Analytic dialectics is a gradual unfolding, unveiling and evolution of Truth, the truth of one's unconscious desire. As Lacan poetically puts it:

> In the recourse of subject to subject that we preserve, psychoanalysis may accompany the patient to the ecstatic limit of the '*Thou art that*', in which is revealed to him the cipher of his mortal destiny, but it is not in our mere power as practitioners to bring him to that point where the real journey begins [Lacan, 1966 [1949], p. 7].

Needless to say, because the Real always returns to the same place (Freud's "repetition compulsion"), transformation is transitional and temporary, at times. Where there is progression, there is regression. As such, analytic praxis, as a dialectical procedure, is more Kierkegaardian than Hegelian because it is one of fluidity and process rather than fixture and stability, hence, Heraclitean rather than Parmenidian. Analysis is a process, a process of becoming otherwise. One becomes other but without becoming another being. Static identity is a mirage, a trap, a lure, a lie. We are in a constant state of change and flux, dynamic and unpredictable. As Heraclitus said, change is the only reality. That is why the third stage of synthesis always comes as a surprise, as a shock to the system, as an epiphanic revelation to the subject whose registers are loss, fragmentation, lack, discontinuity and whose effects reverberate in an endless chain of semiosis, of signifieds slipping under the bar of the signifier.

In analysis we gradually realise we are nothing. Nothing. No thing. As Lacan observes:

> For if love is giving what one does not have, it is certainly true that the subject can wait to be given it, since the psychoanalyst has nothing else to give him. But he does not even give him this nothing, and it is just as well, and that is why he is paid for this nothing, preferably well paid, in order to show that it would not otherwise be worth much [1977 [1958], p. 255].

Hopefully, in time, our *jouissance* will bleed to death.

The synthesis towards which this book is struggling, will inevitably involve the interpenetration and integration of the diverse yet interrelated psychoanalytic perspectives on pale criminality I have been considering. Much of what the theorists say is similar, though their language, framework, terminology and temperament may differ and so obfuscate such similarities and shared concerns. One danger in dialectics is for the synthesis to be reached without the subject undergoing the long, demanding, hermeneutic detour required in which what is familiar conjoins with what is foreign, and both positions are redressed and overcome. Some subjects will avoid working through conflictual antinomies by proclaiming an all-too-sudden and false resolution. Some will fall into the eclectic trap. Dialectics must not be allowed to dissolve into a feeble and facile eclecticism. Furthermore, there will never be one simple or single synthesis, but a plurality and polysemy of possible syntheses.

From confluence and clashes, new modes of being and behaving emerge, pointing, perhaps, towards a new reign of Truth and a new foundation in the wake of destruction, as Heidegger prophesied.

A synthesis

Thus far, at least in the first five chapters, we have adumbrated a largely descriptive and summarised presentation of the psychoanalytic theories of Freud, Jung, Klein, Winnicott and Lacan, and incorporated both orthodox and evolutionary psychiatric perspectives pertaining to "antisocial personality disorder", none of which has been carried out before. In this final chapter, an attempt will be made at synthesising the different analytic approaches, teasing them out, comparing and contrasting them, evaluating and appraising the discoveries yielded so far, and emphasising their respective and relative strengths and weaknesses. Like the last chapter, this chapter aims to be more critical and less expository in nature and scope. Up until now, we have offered an *elucidation* of the various psychoanalytic perspectives on pale criminality; now we must advance an *evaluation* of them.

We have seen how Freud emphasised the unconscious guilt of the pale criminal and the need to be punished deriving from the Oedipus complex. The pale criminal commits a crime or misdeed to mitigate his sense of guilt. Freud sees unconscious guilt as the motive for crime. It is this guilt which induces pale criminals to seek punishment. Rosy criminals, on the other hand, express no remorse, show no guilt. For Freud, the vast majority of criminals were pale ones.

For Freud, guilt derives from the Oedipus complex and is a reaction to the murderous phantasies entertained at this stage. This is supported (psychoanalytically speaking) by Klein, Winnicott and Lacan, though for Klein the Oedipus complex occurs at a much earlier date than it does for Freud. Jung omits mention of the Oedipus complex in relation to criminality and his conceptualisations on this complex differ from Freud's, especially in his consideration of it in terms of its symbolic and spiritual rather than purely sexual significance. In his writings on Dostoevsky, Freud considered *three* characterological traits to be essential to the criminal's structure: egoism, a strong destructive urge and absence of love or, to put it in other words, lack of an emotional appreciation of human objects. This concurs with Winnicott's insight and seems to be borne out in the case histories of certain criminals, in which the time of childhood is crucial (see Masters, 1997 and Canter, 1995). In

Freud's conceptualisations, the Oedipal child internalises his aggression so it is directed to his own ego where it is subsumed by the superego. The tensions provided by the conflict between ego and superego are lacking, so their aggression is directed outwards instead. As conceived by Freud, the hypothesis of a death drive refers to the organism's attempt to reduce excitations and tensions to zero by achieving an inorganic state, as in death for example. To begin with, the death instincts are directed inwards and tend towards self-destruction, as we have already noted, and then subsequently turned towards the outside world in the form of an aggressive and destructive instinct.

Klein viewed the often violent crimes committed by adult criminals as resembling the unconscious phantasy wishes of children which are externalised due to unconscious guilt. She is mostly in agreement with Freud, though she deepens, and in some places markedly departs from, some key Freudian tenets in her description of the internal life of infants, as we have sought to show in chapter three.

Winnicott follows on from Klein, though he emphasises environmental and external factors much more than the child's phantasies about the good and bad breast. Winnicott's position is close to the psychiatric diagnostic of "antisocial personality disorder". His main insight is that emotional deprivation is the cause of delinquency and crime.

Unlike Winnicott, Klein viewed the infant as potentially destructive and violent from birth and stressed the importance of innate, constitutional factors. The view that there are inborn differences between babies, in that one may be more placid and calm while another is more aggressive and violent, has been borne out by contemporary child developmental psychology, and is in substantial agreement with Jung's archetypal hypothesis. Most analysts would say that it is a case of nature and nurture, an interplay, interaction and exchange between society and structure, constitutionality and environment. Environmental frustration (à la Winnicott) as well as innate factors (à la Klein and Jung) are both sources of infantile aggression and rage. But aggression need not be seen solely in the negative light in which Freud tended to view it. Klein, Winnicott and Jung have all emphasised the positive features and aspects inherent in aggression, in that it is the source of mastery, exploration of the environment and intellectual and creative achievement.

Both Klein and Jung emphasise that the murderous potential in all of us is a necessary and crucial part of our biological make-up. Indeed, Adler believed that the "striving for superiority" was the dominant motive of human beings, but like Freud he emphasised a single rather than a plurality of motivations. When Freud finally recognised that there was an aggressive instinct (not solely a sexual one) in man, he concluded that it was primarily self-destructive. Klein and Winnicott have shown that it is connected and directed to mastery of the external world. As Aristotle noted, to exist is to act. What this metaphysical statement means is that we are not born to be stoical spectators standing on the side-lines like passive puppets. Rather, we are passionate participators in the drama of being. We seek activity not passivity. "Act", in Aristotle's sense, is employed in two ways. Act means action but also involves the actualisation of our potentialities. It seems to be in accord with Jung's notion of individuation as a biologically and morally innate imperative.

Klein is to be congratulated for alerting us to the ubiquity of aggression, which she conceived to be operative within the infant from the earliest beginnings of life, but it is nearly impossible to test Kleinian concepts as they pertain so much to unconscious phantasy. Many of her conceptualisations, such as the paranoid–schizoid and depressive positions, are surmised from later anamnetic recollections of children and adults in analysis, rather than from direct observation of children. But direct observation would tell us very little about the unconscious factors anyway, although it would be important in the light of behavioural changes and permutations. After taking into account the fact that memory is an unreliable guide, the additional problem here is that these phantasies occur at a time when the infant is without speech, so at best they must remain as an explanatory hypothesis and at worst as an adult's projection, as Lacan would argue. The truth is that we simply cannot know what is happening in these preverbal stages of infantile development because the infantile subject is lacking in speech. Although it must remain at the level of conjecture, of course, it may still be true.

If Jung held that we are all capable of crime, that we are all repressed criminals possessing the potential and predisposition to crime, Klein too, for her part, maintained that criminal tendencies were present in every "normal" child. Jung alerted us to the dual nature of the criminal, to the "second self" that commits the crimes, which frequently creep up on man, taking hold of him unexpectedly. Klein concurs that there is a fight raging between the cultural and primitive parts of the personality—Freud's Eros battling against its everlasting enemy—Thanatos. And as we have said, for Klein there is a constitutional basis for aggression. She considers that enjoyment and the gratitude to which it gives rise helps to mitigate envious and destructive impulses in general. The feeling of gratitude, for Klein, is a derivative of the capacity for love, which Winnicott termed the "capacity for concern", and which is closely linked up with trust. Gratitude is inexorably bound up with generosity. However, due to the guilt arising from the experience of such anger and destruction and due to massive projection of this aggression, the subject will begin to feel more persecuted and guilty, and the more paranoid and guilty he becomes, the more aggressive he behaves. The subject's own internal aggressor, his superego, which has turned severe, may actually cause him to commit crime. In the above account, we see the close link between criminality and paranoia (phantasies of persecution), which has been borne out in studies on criminals and stressed by both Lacan and Winnicott.

According to Kleinian conceptualisations, criminality is more likely to come from subjects who have not distinguished their first object securely and, hence, cannot distinguish between good and bad. Klein alerts us to the clinical analogy between criminal acts and childish phantasies. In one of the case histories she analysed, a young boy of twelve who had a history of stealing and sexual promiscuity, had no father (he had died), was sexually abused and had been in foster care. All these factors are typical and concur with the findings of Winnicott and the findings of psychiatry. Winnicott, likewise, traces the aetiology of delinquency to specific emotional deprivations in early childhood, directly associating emotional deprivation with delinquency. It is important here, before proceeding, to make a point in logic. Just because most delinquents (criminals) have suffered emotional deprivation does not mean that all those who have experienced emotional deprivation will inevitably become criminals. Because grass is green, it does not mean that green is grass.

Winnicott sees emotional and familial factors as decisive and stresses the positive aspects of delinquency in that it often comes as a cry for help. But the single most important cause of potential criminality lies in the child's prolonged separation from its mother. This is seen as the single most outstanding aetiological factor. Like Klein, he feels that some aggression is innate and like Klein, Jung and Lacan, he draws our attention to the asociality of the criminal. The delinquent child is antisocial, impulsive and does not play; rather, he acts out. Winnicott links destruction with anger and frustration as well as hate and fear. For Winnicott, aggression and destruction are both a reaction to frustration and deprivation and a positive source of energy. He reveals a pattern at work: things go well enough for the child until something disturbs this, the child is then taxed beyond capacity and so is forced to recognise himself on the basis of a new though inferior pattern of ego defence. He then becomes hopeful again and engages in antisocial acts in the hope of coercing society to return with him to the time when things went wrong so as to acknowledge that fact. If this is achieved, the child can return to the period before the moment of deprivation and rediscover the good object or the good enough environment. Here, the mother's role is crucial. Jung also mentions that "lack of love" is the primary mainspring for "violence and terror", and that no-one sets out to hurt others unless they themselves have been hurt.

For Winnicott, *emotional* rather than social deprivation disturbs stable and healthy emotional development and typically occurs in the period of late infancy (from one to two years). In such cases, the personality structure is not fully integrated. At this stage, too, the subject is seeking for parental authority and needs a "strict and strong" father, in Winnicott's words, which is in full agreement with the Lacanian stress on the *nom/non du père*. Furthermore, Winnicott discovers *two* trends in the antisocial behaviour of children: stealing and lying (and destructive acts in general) which accords with the *DSM* diagnostic. Although it is by now obvious that the first few years are paramount, they are by no means of such overriding importance that there are not further developmental stages which are tentative, tenuous and liable to exert tremendous pressure on the individuating subject, (in Jung's terms), that is to say, puberty and adolescence; a period which Winnicott describes as a time of *doldrums*, possessing violent potential and characterised by the *two* aspects of defiance and dependency.

In terms of a possible criminal diagnostic, like Lacan and Klein, Winnicott does not hold to a distinct morphological nosology; he does not view criminality as comparable with neurosis or psychosis. According to Winnicott, the antisocial tendency may be found in so-called normal subjects or in one who is neurotic or psychotic. To this list, both Klein and Lacan would add perversity. Winnicott sees dissociation, denial and disintegration as representing some of the psychological characteristics of the delinquent as, indeed, does Jung. Finally, in terms of treatment, Winnicott says that some form of psychological treatment, though not necessarily psychoanalysis, (a point on which Jung agrees), is essential for the criminal subject, together with punishment, though he opines that the latter is not likely to be very effective. On this note, too, Jung concurs. According to Jung, punishment is necessary, not leniency, in dealing with criminals as prisoners do not improve.

There are many covert similarities between Lacan and Winnicott on the subject of pale criminality and, indeed, between Lacan and Klein. Klein, Winnicott, Bowlby and Lacan all stress the Oedipus complex, the family and the subject's place in the family structure and the presence of unconscious guilt in the criminal who is searching, in his own way, for punishment because his superego demands it. Lacan alerts us to psychopathology whose effects derive precisely from the Oedipus complex and from a dehiscence in the family structure. Like Klein and Winnicott, Lacan links criminality with paranoia, viewing violent crimes in terms of a self-punishing *passage à l'acte* and implies that there are different forms of criminality—neurotic, psychotic and perverse. However, unlike Klein and Winnicott, Lacan stresses the often neglected role of the name-of-the-father (the paternal metaphor) and the importance of his laying down the law. Together with Jung, Klein and Winnicott, Lacan points to the asocial nature of the criminal subject who places himself outside the structures of the Symbolic order acting, as he does, in the Real, though in a symbolic manner. Similarly, in Jung's conceptualisations, the criminal acts in the twilight zone, in a liminal nether region of the night. Finally, Lacan stresses the *structural* side of criminality, corresponding to the aggressivity set up at and stemming from the "mirror stage", but also the symbolic and societal (anthropological) dimensions of criminality.

Jung was the first analytical clinician to apply experimental psychology to criminals, in the form of the word association tests, revealing the complexes underlying the crime. He showed how some criminals try to escape the urge to commit crime by taking refuge in illness. Another way of mitigating the full force of the crime is, according to Jung, by transferring the criminal instincts to others so that they carry out the misdeeds, unconsciously and by proxy, as it were.

Jung assumes that if we blindly follow our passions we inevitably come to the place of the criminal. It is, in fact, all too easy. What is difficult but absolutely necessary is to acknowledge this potential for crime lurking in human nature itself and seek to own it by assimilating our shadow-sides to consciousness, which is, in the last resort, our only redemption. Integration can only occur when our repressed criminality is acknowledged and owned. Left to its own devices, it works evil. Moral effort and moral imagination, for which Iris Murdoch argued, is required in order for us to become conscious of the Shadow, of the dark part of the personality, which shuts out the light. For the Jungian, the choice is stark but simple: Consciousness or absolute Shadow.

Jung humbly acknowledged that he could not say much about murderers and other criminals, pale or rosy, as they did not come to him for analysis. Nor really can we. *By and large*, the criminal does not consult the analyst. Few analysts work in prisons. I felt, however, that an attempt had to be made to understand the structure of the pale criminal subject from the psychoanalytic perspectives, insights and experiences of the most outstanding figures in our discipline of psychoanalysis. The reader will ultimately judge if such an attempt was successful or not. Some questions, of course, remain and must remain. However, in the light of such a synthesis and in conclusion, I set out below *seven psychodynamic* factors pertaining to the pale criminal.

1. Unresolved Oedipus complex.
2. Lack of formation or arrested development of the "moral complex".
3. A severe superego.
4. Unconscious guilt and the attendant need to be punished.

5. Moral masochism.
6. Ego defences such as denial, dissociation or derealisation.
7. A neurotic or perverse structure.

Such, then, are the intrapsychic dynamics involved in the pale criminal's structure.

CONCLUDING NOTE

"While I was sitting on a log, looking down the road the way that I had come, a man came in sight riding on a good-looking horse. The very moment I saw him, I was determined to have his horse. I arose and drew an elegant rifle pistol on him and ordered him to dismount. He did so, and I took his horse by the bridle and pointed down the creek, and ordered him to walk before me. He went a few hundred yards and stopped. I made him undress himself. He said, 'If you are determined to kill me, let me have time to pray before I die.' I told him I had no time to hear him pray. He dropped to his knees, and I shot him through the back of the head. I ripped open his belly and took out his entrails, and sunk him in the creek"

> Jorge Luis Borges, "The Dread Redeemer Lazarus Morell",
> *A Universal History of Infamy*

Throughout this book, but particularly in the ultimate chapter, I have striven to make the point that we need, indeed require, *all* the psychoanalytic perspectives on pale criminality if we are to gain a more complete and correct vision of the pale criminal's structure than would otherwise have been possible if *one* approach had been examined exclusively, and to the detriment of the rest. Each theorist we explored expanded on the work of another, adding, refining and contributing something new and significant to our understanding of the clinical field of pale criminality. One single interpretation is not sufficient because it is, as all interpretations are, perspectival and, hence, incomplete. In this book, I attempted to include the whole spectrum of the major psychoanalytic writings on pale criminality, as no single theory can adequately explain the essential meaning of any phenomenon, which is always in need of further elaboration and amplification.

Each chapter offers a cornucopia of information which, put together, considerably adds to our understanding of the pale criminal's structure. There is, as hermeneuticians such as Paul Ricoeur tell us, no one canon for the correct exegetical reading of cultural phenomena but disparate, opposed and competing claims. There is always a *conflict* of interpretations. We have tried to arbitrate between each interpretation and the reader will have to judge for himself which one is the most convincing. Alternatively, he can draw on a plurality of perspectives. I argue that there is no one, final, true interpretation, hence the selection of several analytical strands in this work. Hermeneutically, one always remains caught within the confines of the hermeneutic circle where meaning is always indirect, multivocal and gained only through the *hermeneutic detour* of differing interpretations—be they Freudian, Jungian, Kleinian, Winnicottian, Lacanian, psychiatric etc. Such a reading, as I have offered, resists absolute or ultimate knowledge and triumphalistic, superior vantage points of complete lucidity where everything is fully explained and, hence, forever understood. The unconscious bars absolute knowledge.

I hope that, in terms of epistemology, my dialectical approach is deemed worthwhile and the final outcome, now that we have come full circle, regarded as representing a successful and convincing synthesis on the subject of the pale criminal and his structure.

Reflecting on this research, which saw the application of psychoanalytic theories to pale criminality, I have realised the extent to which I have mainly emphasised the *structural* rather than the sociological criteria pertaining to pale criminality; in other words, the intrapsychic and subjective dimension as distinct from intersubjective and social relations. This work has also indirectly challenged the notion of *social* deprivation as the primary cause of crime, much beloved of the political Left.

Following upon these analytic insights, I think one could say that, in Lacanian terminology, criminality can be understood, amongst other things, as representing a rage against the Symbolic order and repudiation of the Name-of-the-Father, a disavowal of the paternal function, a lapse of the Law. This kind of subject resists the father's account (*verse au père—père-version*). He negates, denies, transgresses and repudiates the structures of the Symbolic.

The criminal subject, acting in the Real in a symbolic way, is a stray on a journey through the night, travelling the way of the shadow. He has a sense of danger and risk. "And the more he strays, the more he is saved" (Kristeva, 1982, p. 8). Why? Because out of such straying "on excluded ground" (ibid.), the criminal draws his *jouissance*. He neither knows nor desires it. He simply joys in it (*on en jouit*), playfully, passionately, violently. Refusing, rejecting, repelling, rebelling. The criminal acknowledges the impossibility of the Law, of Morality, of Religion. He transgresses and refuses these ideals. Criminality represents, then, the collapse of paternal laws.

The criminal, situated as he is outside the structures of the Symbolic, is not social. Rather, he is profoundly antisocial. He disrupts the Symbolic order, disturbing the system, not respecting "borders, positions, rules" (ibid. p. 4). He is, in Jung's words, "a moral exile", (Jung, 1934–1939, p. 1453) haunted by his misdeeds. He is the robber, the rapist, the torturer, the terrorist, the traitor, the killer. He sets up his depraved desire against the Symbolic (paternal) law, which he loathes. He acts on the nether side of the Name (of-the-father), which never said No.

Like all human subjects, the criminal had a choice and he *chose* to be a criminal and so to live in a liminal state away from the light. The criminal, drawing his *jouissance* from his crimes, lives in a land of darkness, blackness, heaviness. For the shadow the criminal casts consumes him and he himself becomes the ashes.

REFERENCES

Abrahamsen, D. (1960). *The Psychology of Crime*. Columbia University Press.

Alexander, F. (1938). Remarks about the relation of inferiority feelings to guilt feelings. *International Journal of Psycho-Analysis*, 19: 41–49.

Alexander, F., & Staub, H. (1931) *The Criminal, the Judge, and the Public*. London: George Allen and Unwin.

Althusser, L. (1994). *The Future Lasts A Long Time and the Facts*. Trans. Richard Veasey. New Jersey: Vintage.

Asch, S. A. (1975). Some superego considerations in crime and punishment. In: *The Psychoanalytic Forum*, vol. 5. New York: International Universities Press.

Augustine, S. (1992). *Confessions*. Trans. Henry Chadwick. *The World's Classics. Saint Augustine. Confessions*. Oxford & New York: Oxford University Press.

Axelrod, R., & Hamilton, W. D. (1981). The evolution of co-operation. *Science*, 211: 1390–1396.

Banville, J. (1989). *The Book of Evidence*. London: Minerva.

Bienenfeld, F. R. (1957). Justice, aggression and eros. *International Journal of Psycho-Analysis*, 32: 419–427.

Bion, W. (1955a). Language and the schizophrenic. In: *New Directions in Psycho-Analysis*. London: Tavistock Publications.

Bion, W. (1955b). Differentiation of the psychotic from the non-psychotic personalities. *International Journal of Psycho-Analysis*, 38.

Bion, W. (1959). Attacks on linking. *International Journal of Psycho-Analysis*, 40.

Blomeyer, R. (1982). *Der Spiele der Analytiker: Freud, Jung und die Analyse*. Walter: Olten.

Borges, J. L. (1975). The Dread Redeemer Lazarus Morell. In: *A Universal History of Infamy*. Trans. Norman Thomas di Giovanni. London: Penguin Books.

Bowlby, J. (1940). The influence of early environment in the development of neurosis and neurotic character. *International Journal of Psycho-Analysis*, 21.

Bowlby, J. (1951). *Maternal Care and Mental Health*. Geneva: WHO; London: HMSO; New York: Columbia University Press.

Bowlby, J. (1958). The Nature of the Child's Tie to his Mother. *International Journal of Psycho-Analysis*, 39: 350–373.

Bowlby, J. (1969). *Attachment and Loss. Vol 1: Attachment*. London: Hogarth Press.

Bowlby, J. (1973). *Attachment and Loss. Vol. 2: Separation, Anxiety and Anger*. London: Hogarth Press.

Bowlby, J. (1979). *The Making and Breaking of Affectional Bonds*. London: Tavistock Publications.

Camus, A. (1982 [1942]). *The Outsider*. Trans. Joseph Laredo. London: Penguin Books.

Canter, D. (1995). *Criminal Shadows*. London: Harper Collins Publishers.

Carvalho, R. (1982). Parental deprivation in relation to narcissistic danger. *Journal of Analytical Psychology*, 27(4): 341–356.

Céline, L-F. (1966). *Death On The Installment Plan*. Trans. Ralph Manheim. New York: New Directions Books.

Chance, M. R. A., & Jolly, C. (1970). *Social Groups of Monkeys: Apes and Men*. New York and London: Jonathon Capes/E.P. Dutton.

Costello, S. J. (1995). Freud's moral psychology and its implications for philosophical ethics. *Journal of the Irish Forum for Psychoanalytic Psychotherapy*, 5(1&2): Spring/Autumn.

Costello, S. J. (1996). Lacan and the lure of the look. In: *The Letter: Lacanian Perspectives on Psychoanalysis*. Autumn.

Costello, S. J. (1997a). What type of knowledge? The Fideist position in psychoanalytic praxis. *The Letter*, Spring.

Costello, S. J. (1997b). The pale criminal and the need for punishment: A Freudian perspective. *The Letter*, Autumn.

Costello, S. J. (1998). Klein's little criminals. *Journal of the Irish Forum for*

Psychoanalytic Psychotherapy, Spring.

Dixon, D. J. (1986). On the criminal mind: An imaginary lecture by Sigmund Freud. *International Journal of Offender Therapy and Comparative Criminology*, 30(2): 101–109.

Dostoyevsky, F. (1991). *Crime and Punishment*. London: Penguin.

DSM-IV: *Diagnostic and Statistical Manual of Mental Disorders*, 4th edition (1994). American Psychiatric Association, Washington.

Duxbury, N. (1989). Exploring legal tradition: Psychoanalytic theory and Roman law in modern continental jurisprudence. *Legal Studies*, 9(1): 84–98.

East, W. N. (1949). *Society and the Criminal*. London: His Majesty's Stationary Office.

Ehrenzweig, A. A. (1964). A psychoanalysis of the insanity plea. *Yale Law Journal*, 73: 425–441.

Ellis, B. E. (1991). *American Psycho*. London: Picador.

Erikson, E. (1951). *Childhood and Society*. London: Imago.

Feldman, P. (1993). *The Psychology of Crime*. USA: Cambridge University Press.

Fenichel, O. (1928). The clinical aspect of the need for punishment. *International Journal of Psychoanalysis*, 9: 47–70.

Flugel, J. C. (1945). *Man, Morals and Society: A Psychoanalytic Study*. London: Butler and Tanner.

Fordham, M. (1957). *New Developments in Analytical Psychology*. London: Routledge and Kegan Paul.

Foucault, M. (1991). *Discipline and Punish: The Birth of the Clinic*. Trans. Alan Sheridan. London: Penguin.

Fox, R. (1989). *The Search for Society: Quest for a Biosocial Science and Morality*. New Brunswick and London: Rutgers University Press.

Freud, S. (1906). Psycho-analysis and the establishment of the facts in legal proceedings. *S.E.*, 9.

Freud, S. (1912–1913). *Totem and Taboo*. *S.E.*, 7.

Freud, S. (1916). Some character types met with in psycho-analytic work. *S.E.*, 14.

Freud, S. (1916–1917). The development of the libido and the sexual organizations. *Introductory Lectures on Psycho-Analysis*. *S.E.*, 16.

Freud, S. (1920). The psychogenesis of a case of homosexuality in a woman. *S.E.*, 18: 145–172.

Freud, S. (1921). *Group Psychology and the Analysis of the Ego*. *S.E.*, 14.

Freud, S. (1923). *The Ego and the Id*. *S.E.*, 19.

Freud, S. (1924a). The dissolution of the Oedipus complex. *S.E.*, 19.

Freud, S. (1924b). The economic problem of masochism. *S.E., 19.*

Freud, S. (1925). Preface to Aichorn's 'Wayward Youth'. *S.E., 19.*

Freud, S. (1927). *The Future of an Illusion. S.E., 21.*

Freud, S. (1928). Dostoevsky and parricide. *S.E., 21.*

Freud, S. (1930). *Civilization and Its Discontents. S.E., 21.*

Freud, S. (1931). The expert opinion in the Halsmann case. *S.E., 21.*

Freud, S. (1933). The dissection of the psychical personality. Lecture xxxi, *New Introductory Lectures On Psycho-Analysis. S.E., 22.*

Freud, S. (1939). *Moses and Monotheism. S.E., 23.*

Freud, S. (1953–1974). *The Standard Edition of the Complete Psychological Works of Sigmund Freud.* Trans. James Stratchey, in collaboration with Anna Freud. London: The Hogarth Press. Entries listed according to date of original writing and volume.

Glover, E. (1956). Psychoanalysis and criminology: a political survey. *International Journal of Psycho-Analysis,* 37: 311–317.

Glover, E. (1960). *The Roots of Crime.* London: Imago Publishing Company.

Goldstein, J. (1968). Psychoanalysis and Jurisprudence. *Yale Law Journal,* 77(6): 1053–1077.

Glantz, K., & Pearce, J. (1989). *Exiles from Eden: Psychotherapy From an Evolutionary Perspective.* New York: Norton.

Hale, N. G. (1995). *The Rise and Crisis of Psychoanalysis in the United States: Freud and the Americans, 1917–1985.* New York–Oxford: Oxford University Press.

Harpending, H. C., & Sobus, J. (1987). Sociopathy as an adaptation. *Ethology and Sociobiology,* 8(35): 63–72.

Hegel, G. W. F. (1977). *Phenomenology of Spirit.* Trans. A. V. Miller. Oxford–New York–Toronto–Melbourne. London: Oxford University Press.

Henry, J. (1977). Comment on 'The cerebral hemisphere in analytical psychology by Rossi, E'. *Journal of Analytical Psychology,* 22(2): 52–58.

Herzog, E., & Sudia, C. (1970). *Boys in Fatherless Families.* Washington, DC: US Department of Health, Education and Welfare.

Joseph, B. (1960). Some characteristics of the psychopathic personality. *International Journal of Psycho-Analysis,* 41: 526–531.

Jung, C. G. Most quotations in the text are taken from *The Collected Works of C. G. Jung.* Edited by H. Read, M. Fordham and G. Adler, and published in London by Routledge and Kegan Paul, 1953–1978, in New York by Pantheon Books, 1953–1960, and the Bollingen Foundation, 1961–1967, and in Princeton, New Jersey, 1967–1978.

Quotation sources are indicated by the volume number followed by the number of the paragraph from which the quotation is taken (e.g., *CW* 12, para. 122). Sources other than *The Collected Works* are listed below.

Jung, C. G. (1933). *Modern Man in Search of a Soul*. London: Kegan Paul.

Jung, C. G. (1988). *Nietzsche's Zarathustra: Notes of the Seminar given in 1934–1939 by C. G. Jung*. Ed. James L. Jarrett. In Two Parts. London: Routledge.

Jung, C. G. (1995). *Memories, Dreams, Reflections*. Edited and recorded by Aniela Jaffé. Trans. Richard and Clara Winston. London: Fontana Press.

Kaplan, L. V. (1967). An academic lawyer plays armchair analyst: Some speculations on the relevance of psychoanalysis to the law. *Nebraska Law Review*, 46(4): 759–797.

Klein, M. (1927). Criminal tendencies in normal children. *Love, Guilt and Reparation, and Other Works, 1921–1945* (pp. 110–185). London: Virago Press, 1988.

Klein, M. (1928). Early stages of the Oedipus conflict. In: *Love, Guilt And Reparation and Other Works 1921–1945*. London: Virago Press, 1988.

Klein, M. (1932). *The Psycho-Analysis of Children*. Trans. Alix Stratchey. London: Virago Press, 1989.

Klein, M. (1933). The early development of conscience in the child. In: *Love, Guilt and Reparation, and Other Works, 1921–1945*. London: Virago Press, 1988.

Klein, M. (1934). On criminality. In: *Love, Guilt and Reparation and Other Works, 1921–1945*. London: Virago Press, 1988.

Klein, M. (1935). A contribution to the psychogenesis of manic–depressive states. In: *Love, Guilt And Reparation and Other Works 1921–1945*. London: Virago Press, 1988.

Klein, M. (1940). Mourning and its relation to manic–depressive states. In: *Love, Guilt And Reparation and Other Works 1921–1945*. London: Virago Press, 1988.

Klein, M. (1945). The Oedipus complex in the light of early anxieties. In: *Love, Guilt And Reparation and Other Works 1921–1945* (pp. 370–419). London: Virago Press, 1988.

Klein, M. (1946). Notes on some schizoid mechanisms. In: *Envy And Gratitude, and Other Works 1946–1963*. London: Virago Press, 1988.

Klein, M. (1955). On identification. In: *Envy And Gratitude, and Other Works 1946–1963*. London: Virago Press, 1988.

Klein, M. (1957). Envy and gratitude. In: *Envy and Gratitude, and Other*

Works 1946–1963. London: Virago Press, 1988.

Klein, M. (1963). Some reflections on '*The Oresteia*'. In: *Envy and Gratitude, and Other Works 1946–1963*. London: Virago Press,1988.

Kristeva, J. (1982). *Powers of Horror: An Essay on Abjection*. Trans. Leon S. Roudiez. New York: Columbia University Press.

Lacan, J. (1938). *The Family Complexes in the Formation of the Individual*. Unpublished. Trans. Cormac Gallagher, School of Psychotherapy, St. Vincent's Hospital, 1982.

Lacan, J. (1957–1958). *Le Séminaire. Livre v. Les formations de l'inconscient, 1957–58* (unpublished). Trans. Cormac Gallagher, *The Formations of the Unconscious, 1957–58*. (Includes 'The Paternal Metaphor I'.)

Lacan, J. (1966). Introduction Théorique aux Fonctions de la Psychanalyse en Criminologie (1950), *Écrits*. Paris: Editions du Seuil, 1966. Trans. Mark Bracker, Russell Grigg and Robert Samuels. A theoretical introduction to the functions of psychoanalysis in criminology. *Journal for the Psychoanalysis of Culture and Society*, 1(2) Autumn, 1996, pp. 13–25.

Lacan, J. (1973) The problem of style and the psychiatric conception of paranoic forms of experience. *Critical Texts*, 5.3.

Lacan, J. *The Seminar of Jacques Lacan. Book X. Anxiety, 1962–63* (unpublished). Trans. C. Gallagher.

Lacan, J. *Le Séminaire. Livre xv. L'Acte Psychanalytique, 1967–68* (unpublished). Trans. C. Gallagher.

Lacan, J. (1972–73). *Le Séminaire. Livre xx. Encore, 1972–73*, ed. Jacques-Alain Miller. Paris: Seuil.

Lacan, J. (1975). *Le Séminaire. Livre i. Les écrits technique de Freud, 1953–4*, ed. Jacques-Alain Miller. Paris: Seuil.

Lacan, J. (1975–1976). *Le Séminaire. Livre xxiii. Le sinthome, 1975–76*, published in *Ornicar?*, nos. 6–11, 1976–7.

Lacan, J. (1977a). The function and field of speech and language in psychoanalysis (1953). In: *Écrits: A Selection*. Trans. Alan Sheridan. London: Routledge.

Lacan, J. (1977b). The mirror stage as formative of the function of the I as revealed in psychoanalytic experience (1949). In: *Écrits: A Selection*. Trans. Alan Sheridan. London: Routledge.

Lacan, J. (1977c). Tuché and automaton. In: *The Four Fundamental Concepts of Psycho-Analysis*. Trans. Alan Sheridan. London: Penguin Books.

Lacan, J. (1981). *Le Séminaire. Livre iii. Les Psychoses, 1955–56*, ed. Jacques-Alain Miller. Paris: Seuil.

Lacan, J. (1982). Intervention on the transference. Trans. Jacqueline

Rose. In: Juliet Mitchell & Jacqueline Rose (Eds), *Feminine Sexuality: Jacques Lacan and the école freudienne* (pp. 61–73). London: Macmillan.

Lacan, J. (1987). *The Seminar. Book 1. Freud's Papers on Technique, 1953–54.* Trans. John Forrester. Cambridge University Press.

Lacan, J. (1988). *The Seminar. Book ii. The Ego in Freud's Theory and in the Technique of Psychoanalysis, 1954–55.* Trans. Sylvana Tomaselli. Cambridge: Cambridge University Press.

Lacan, J. (1992). *The Ethics of Psychoanalysis 1959–1960. The Seminar of Jacques Lacan. Book vii.* Trans. Dennis Porter. London: Tavistock/Routledge.

Lacan, J. (1993). *The Seminar. Book iii. The Psychoses, 1955–56.* Trans. Russell Grigg. London: Routledge.

Levinson, D. (1978). *The Seasons of a Man's Life.* New York: Knopf.

Lumsden, C. J., & Wilson, E. O. (1983). *Promethean Fire: Reflections on the Origin of Mind.* Cambridge, Mass. & London: Harvard University Press.

Maduro, R., & Wheelwright, J. (1977). Analytical psychology. In: R. Corsimi (Ed.), *Current Personality Theories.* Itasca: Peacock.

Mailer, N. (1991). *The Executioner's Song.* London: Vintage.

Masters, B. (1997). *The Evil that Men Do.* London: Black Swan.

Mednick, S., & Christiansen, K. (1977). *Biosocial Bases of Criminal Behaviour.* New York: Gardner.

Meninger, K. (1968). *The Crime of Punishment.* USA: Penguin.

Midgley, M. (1979). *Beast and Man: The Roots of Human Nature.* Sussex: Harvester Press.

Mullins, C. (1943). *Crime and Psychology.* London: Methuen and Co.

Neumann, E. (1955). *The Great Mother: An Analysis of the Archetype.* London: Routledge and Kegan Paul.

Neumann, E. (1973). *The Child.* London: Hodder and Staughton.

Nietzsche, F. (1961). Of the Pale Criminal, Zarathustra's Discourses. In: *Thus Spake Zarathustra.* Trans. R. J. Hollingdale. London: Penguin.

Poe, Edgar Allan (1986). The Murders in the Rue Morgue. In: *The Fall of the House of Asher and Other Writings.* London: Penguin.

Rappaport, R. G. (1988). The serial and mass murderer: patterns, differentiation, pathology. *The American Journal of Forensic Psychiatry*, 9(1): 38–48.

Reik, T. (1936). *The Unknown Murderer.* London: Hogarth Press and The Institute of Psychoanalysis.

Rimbaud, A. (1962). *A Season in Hell.* Trans. Oliver Bernard. London: Penguin Books.

Rossi, E. (1977). The cerebral hemisphere in analytical psychology. *Journal of Analytical Psychology*, 22(1): 32–58.

Samuels, A. (1982). The image of the parents in bed. *Journal of Analytical Psychology*, 27(4): 323–340.

Samuels, A. (1985). *Jung and the Post-Jungians*. London: Routledge and Kegan Paul.

Seligman, E. (1982). The half-alive ones. *Journal of Analytical Psychology*, 27(1): 1–20.

Staude, J. R. (1981). *The Adult Development of C. G. Jung*. Boston and London: Routledge and Kegan Paul.

Stevens, A. (1982). *Archetype: A Natural History of the Self*. London: Routledge and Kegan Paul.

Stevens, A. (1994). *Jung*. Oxford: Oxford University Press.

Stevens, A. (1995). *Private Myths: Dreams and Dreaming*. London: Penguin.

Stevens, A., & Price, J. (1996). *Evolutionary Psychiatry: A New Beginning*. London and New York: Routledge.

Storr, A. (1968). *Human Aggression*. London: Allen Lane.

Storr, A. (1973). *Jung*. London: Fontana Stykes, Gresham and Cullen, Francis T. 1992 *Criminology*. USA: Harcourt Brace Jovanovich College Publishers.

Tinbergen, N. (1951). *The Study of Instinct*. London: Oxford University Press.

Van der Heydt (1973). On the father in psychotherapy. In: P. Berry (Ed.), *Fathers and Mothers*. Spring, Zurich.

Waddington, C. H. (1957). *The Strategies of the Genes: A Discussion of Some Aspects of Theoretical Biology*. London: George Allen and Unwin.

West, R. (1986). Law, rights, and other totemic illusions: legal liberalism and Freud's theory of the rule of law. *University of Pennsylvania Law Review*, 134(4): 817–882.

White, W. A. (1923). *Insanity and the Criminal Law*. New York: MacMillan.

Williams, H. A. (1960). A psycho-analytic approach to the treatment of the murderer. *International Journal of Psycho-Analysis*, 41: 532–539.

Winnicott, D. W. (1984). *Deprivation and Delinquency*. London: Routledge.

Winnicott, D. W. (1987). Delinquency as a sign of hope. In: *Home Is Where We Start From: Essays by a Psychoanalyst*. London: Pelican Books.

Wollheim, R. (1988). Crime, punishment and pale criminality. *Oxford Journal of Legal Studies*, 8(1): 1–16.

Yarvis, R. M. (1972). A classification of criminal offenders through the use of current psychoanalytic concepts. *The Psychoanalytic Review*, 59(4): 549–563.

Yochelson, S., & Samenow, S. (1976). *The Criminal Personality*, vol. 1: *A Profile for Change*. New York: Jason Aronson.

Zilboorg, G. (1956). The contribution of psychoanalysis to forensic psychiatry. *International Journal of Psycho-Analysis*, 37: 318–324.

INDEX